AN UNARRANGED LIFE

AN
UNARRANGED
LIFE

JAGANNATH WANI

This edition published in 2019 by Raju Wani: Calgary, Canada. wani34ca@gmail.com

Print ISBN 978-1-9990263-0-1
Ebook ISBN 978-1-9990263-1-8

Cover and jacket design by Allen Zuk

Design and production of book and ebook interiors by Stephanie Small and Allen Zuk

In loving memory of my grandmother
Reu Aaji
who taught me unconditional love
by her own example

.

10% of life is made up of what happens to you.
90% of life is decided by how you react.

STEPHEN COVEY

FOREWORD

"When can I go back home?" my Dad asked me from the hospice. He wanted just another six or seven months to live so he could keep helping people, continue making a difference in the world through his various causes, and see this book through to publication. My Dad was a fighter, and I felt broken, because I knew he would never be going home again and that my days with him were numbered. I will always remember his remarkable strength.

My Mom had lost her battle with cancer about five months prior to my Dad's passing. I always told my Dad that I would take care of my Mom if something were to happen to him, yet he was determined to outlive her so that he could take care of her. My Dad had always been an outstanding caregiver during my Mom's lifelong battle with mental illness. He battled stage four colon cancer himself for four and a half years and was on a clinical trial after being on many chemo treatments. He would find the strength to cook for my Mom during this time, fighting his own side effects during her last month. If he didn't know how to cook a dish that my Mom had requested, he would call his sister in India in order to find out how to prepare it. That was the kind of sincere and caring individual that my Dad was—truly one of a kind.

I believe my Dad's passion to help the less fortunate kept him alive. He always told me to take life one day at a time. He took his own advice and was able to accomplish a lot in those four and a half years. He spent the last month of his life in the Carewest Sarcee Hospice in Calgary. The staff at the Hospice were fantastic and provided superb care to my Mom and my Dad during their time at the facility.

My Dad had never wanted me to stay overnight at the Hospice—for the last month, I would arrive in the morning every day and leave only to sleep at night. By May 5th, 2017 my Dad had been in an unconscious state for about a day. I told him I would be staying with him overnight, as his nurse felt he had about 24 hours to a few days left. I told him I would be leaving the room briefly to walk my wife to the car. As I returned to his room, I saw him gasp, and suddenly realized I had witnessed his last breath. I believe he was waiting for me to be with him for his final moment.

To his family he was a great father and grandfather, and to others he was a great role model, a mentor, and a helping hand. I miss him every day.

Raju Wani

INTRODUCTION

In over thirty-five years as a mental health activist, I have met many mentally ill people and their caregivers. I was once shocked to hear, during a public meeting, a caregiver mother saying, "I wish my son had cancer rather than schizophrenia." Another woman wondered, "Why did my husband divorce me when a pill a day, as with diabetes and blood pressure, could have managed my mental illness?" Many patients and caregivers are seeking answers to similar questions.

At least one in one hundred people are diagnosed with schizophrenia. According to the World Health Organization, at any given time, approximately 450 million people worldwide suffer from some form of mental or behavioural disorder. This is an astounding statistic. How can these unfortunate people be helped? A sensitive caregiver makes all the difference. A caregiver with patience, perseverance, and support from a competent psychiatrist can help the unfortunate family members lead a near normal life.

The spouse of a person suffering from mental illness often opts for a divorce. But this option is not available to fathers, mothers, daughters, sons, brothers, or sisters of the mentally ill. The mental illness of a spouse is a socially acceptable ground to seek divorce and find a new partner. But what if the couple has children? Should the healthy parent not think of the future of the children? Living with a mentally ill spouse in order to keep the family intact is a challenging option. This book recounts my own triumphs and tragedies in living with my wife's schizophrenia.

My forty-four years of living with a mentally ill wife and managing her schizophrenia helped me understand the plight of other caregivers. The experience turned me into a mental health activist, working for the mentally ill and their caregivers in Canada and in India. I realized first-hand that the bewildered family of a person with schizophrenia suffers as much as the patient—if not more. A caregiver husband has a manifold challenge in managing his wife's schizophrenia—caring for the children, working as an activist, and, at the same time, acting as the breadwinner and maintaining a professional career. Juggling these roles taught me many lessons in my unarranged life and motivated me to write this book. I sincerely hope it will inspire caregivers to strive for solutions and save families from disintegration.

While learning to care for my wife Kamalini, I had to deal with a number of psychiatrists. The first one I met was based 5000 kilometres away, in New York. He correctly diagnosed my wife's condition as schizophrenia, a disease I'd never heard of before. As per his suggestion I contacted a local psychiatrist for follow-up treatment. The local psychiatrist continued the oral medication first prescribed by the doctor from New York, and when the medication stopped working, he started Kamalini on a round of electroconvulsive therapy. Later, we met with a third psychiatrist during an emergency situation. He advised divorce. Thereafter my wife refused to see a psychiatrist for treatment, and I had no legal recourse available to have her treated against her will. Her condition deteriorated and became physically life-threatening, at which point it became legally possible for me to compel her to be treated. She was admitted to the hospital where I met the fourth psychiatrist, who was on duty at the time. He did not believe in ECT and started Kamalini on injectable medication. In getting to know these various psychiatrists with their differing viewpoints, I learned a great deal about the variety of medications, procedures, and approaches used in the treatment of schizophrenia.

In my role as a mental health activist I've had to dispel many myths about schizophrenia. Does the patient with schizophrenia have a split personality, like Dr. Jekyll and Mr. Hyde? I've also had to counsel care-givers that their own fitness—mental and physical—must take priority. On airplanes, the flight attendants advise you to put on your own oxygen mask first before helping others. If a caregiver himself breaks down, he cannot provide adequate care to the patient.

With equal concern for the wellbeing of the caregiver and of the patient I offer this book, which I hope will acquaint the reader with many issues—medical, emotional, and practical—that arise in the management of schizophrenia.

AN UNARRANGED LIFE

1

AT THE EDGE

In July 1972, my wife Kamalini and I returned home to Calgary after a month-long family vacation in India with our three children. Soon after, our two-year old son Raju fell sick. He was running a high temperature and had become weak and thin. We took him to his pediatrician, who ordered blood tests. At the pathology lab, the technician had hard time finding a vein in his little arm; she kept poking around until Raju cried helplessly. It was an unbearable sight for me and especially for Kamalini. She had tears in her eyes, but she didn't cry.

One evening after dinner the children went into the living room and turned on the TV to watch *Bugs Bunny and Roadrunner*, their favourite cartoon. There was no argument about the selection of the show; it was unanimous. I was helping Kamalini clear the table. Everything was going according to our normal routine. All of a sudden Kamalini turned from loading the dishwasher and whispered,

"Our relatives back home are plotting to harm us."

"What?" I asked in disbelief.

"There is a plot to harm us."

"How do you know?" I asked feeling irritated.

"Raju's sickness is part of the plot."

"That doesn't make sense." I tried to reach around her to open a cupboard. "The harsh summer in India might have caused it."

She was standing very straight with a bowl still in her hand. "My brother Ram used witchcraft and caused Raju's fever."

There was no logic in Kamalini's statements. In my opinion, none of Kamalini's relatives had time to find ways to harm us from a distance of fifteen thousand kilometres. Perhaps some of them were jealous of our comfortable life in Canada; such jealousy is part of human nature. That they were plotting to harm us was a totally unthinkable idea.

Within a few days, Kamalini's list of the "plotters" had expanded to include my father and one of my brothers. But, unlike in the case of her brother, she did not describe the plot hatched by these two new enemies.

"Write letters to all of them," she insisted.

"What do I write?" I asked.

"We are simple and honest people. Some of our relatives are plotting to harm us. With God's grace they will not succeed."

"I can't write any such letters," I said.

"What will we achieve by doing this?"

"Please, do it for my sake," she pleaded.

Believing that the letters might put her mind at peace, I did as she asked. I included exactly the same statements as Kamalini had pronounced. None of the relatives bothered to reply. In hindsight, I realize that I made a fool of myself. But Kamalini was still anxious. A few days later she puzzled me with another statement. We had just finished our breakfast; I was browsing through the morning paper. Picking up the dishes, Kamalini said, "An article in a magazine explains the solution to our problems."

"What problems? We don't have any."

"Get that magazine, and you will know," Kamalini said while wiping the table.

"What's the name of the magazine?"

She looked at me, challengingly. "I don't know, but we could find it."

I stared back at her. I didn't know how to understand her, or how to make her understand that there was no logic in her statements.

On a Friday, later in the month, I returned home after attending a staff meeting at the University of Calgary, where I was an associate professor of Statistics. Our eight-year old daughter, Varsha, opened the door. "Look what Mom's done," she said, pointing to rows of newspaper clippings pasted throughout the hallway and across the doorways to the bedrooms. Kamalini was in the living room watching *Flintstones* cartoons on TV with Sulabha, who was six, and Raju.

"What's the purpose of these newspaper cuttings?" I asked her, gesturing back towards the papers on the walls.

"It looks good. I wanted to decorate the apartment," she responded calmly.

I strolled along the hallway reading the article headings. There was no particular common subject or theme. The display, I believed, was an expression of her delusion of an article in a magazine providing solutions to her imagined problems.

Two weeks after this, I was on my way home after teaching my statistics class at the University. The building manager passed me on my way to the elevators, his usual smile replaced with a look of contempt. I was perplexed until Kamalini told me later, "I summoned the police to our apartment."

I stared at her. "What—when?"

"A few weeks ago"

"Why?"

She lowered her head diffidently. "I wanted help from them."

"For what?"

"To find that magazine," Kamalini quietly responded. "The one with the solution to our problems."

"What did the police say?"

"Go search in a public library." For the first time, she looked unsure of herself.

How could I convince her that there was no such magazine? And if I could convince her, would she be at peace? A week later, after lunch, I dropped her off at the Central Library, Calgary's main public library. She had the whole afternoon to look for the magazine. In the evening I went to pick her up.

"Did you find the magazine?" I asked her as she was getting into the car.

"No. I asked the staff for help."

I couldn't read her expression. "Well? What did they say?"

"They asked for the name of the magazine. But I didn't know the name."

A week later, I was going through a photo album when I noticed a missing photograph.

"Kamal, a photo's missing from this album," I said, as I flipped back and forth through the pages.

"I threw it down the garbage chute," Kamalini said without looking at me, "along with a few other things."

"What other things?"

She shrugged casually. "Two more photos, books, dishes and some clothes."

"Why?" I could feel my frustration rising.

"They were causing me the problem. I had to destroy them."

"But what's your problem?" I asked her, as calmly as I could.

She looked confused. "I don't know."

One of the things that went down the chute was a treatise on the *Dnyaneshwari*. For an educated Marathi-speaking person, the *Dnyaneshwari* is sacred, like the Bible to Christians. It is a commentary on the *Bhagwat Gita*, a part of the epic Mahabharata, authored by the thirteenth-century child saint Dnyaneshwar. Kamalini's brother-in-law, Narayan, had affectionately presented the treatise to me. I was upset but didn't get angry. What would I achieve by getting angry?

Over the next several weeks, Kamalini began using abusive language. "Stop shouting and yelling!" Kamalini would scream.

"I'm not," I would respond.

Once she told me, "You will suffer from leprosy."

I looked into her eyes. "How will that help you?" I asked.

"You will be totally ruined!" Kamalini continued.

"What'll happen to you and the children?"

She clenched her jaw. "Better if you die."

The conversation was always in Marathi. Our children did not understand a word, though they could sense that mom was using foul language. Sulabha once remarked, "Daddy, you should have married a better wife."

The two-bedroom apartment we rented had always been inadequate for the five of us. Instead of buying a house available on the market, we decided to construct a custom-built home. In September 1972, we had purchased a piece of land in Varsity Estates, a neighbourhood close to the university. It was situated at the end of a cul-de-sac, which meant no traffic on the road, and hence a safe place for the children to play. It backed onto an eighteen-hole golf course deep in a ravine. The elementary and junior high schools were within walking distance, and it was just about a five-minute drive to the university, with Market Mall, one of Calgary's largest shopping centres, on the way.

I had a dream about the house we wanted to construct. I prepared a rough sketch and in December 1972 approached a draftsman with the sketch. He transformed my ideas into a set of working drawings. The design included an inviting entrance with a spacious foyer, an open staircase, and a gallery leading to the bedrooms. The foyer was at the centre of it all; it provided access to the living room, the study, kitchen, garage, basement and bedrooms upstairs. The floor plan was open, allowing for free traffic flow all around the main floor. I brought home the bundle with eight pages of drawings neatly rolled and secured with a rubber band.

"What is it, Daddy?" Varsha asked.

"Drawings of our new home," I answered. "It will be much bigger than this apartment."

Varsha reached for the roll of papers. "Can I see?"

"Sure!"

I spread the papers out on the dining table and opened the page showing the bedroom layout. Sulabha and Raju climbed on chairs to see. Though Raju was too young to understand the plans, he was excited. "Will I have my own bedroom, Daddy?"

"Of course you will," I said.

"Which is my bedroom?" asked Sulabha.

"I don't know. We'll decide after the construction is complete." I answered cautiously to avoid any arguments between the children on the selection of their rooms.

Sulabha rushed on. "Will you let me choose the colour for my bedroom?"

"I want green carpet in my room," Varsha announced.

I smiled and gestured at the drawings. "I will give you full choice to make your selections."

Kamalini did not join in the excitement of the children; she just watched and listened, stirring the curry on the stove.

———

Varsha once brought home an origami book from the school library. Kamalini was fascinated with the different figures shown in the book.

On her own she learned the art of folding paper and started to enjoy it. She bought three books on the subject and created wonderful, intricate sculptures such as a flying eagle and an elegant swan. It became her main hobby. One day she challenged Varsha and Sulabha, "If you are so clever, can you do this?" The girls were taken aback by the question. They didn't know how to respond.

Sulabha resented her mother's behaviour, refusing to go out shopping if Kamalini was going to accompany us. The weekly shopping trip had to be divided into two sessions—grocery shopping with Kamalini while the girls were in school, and shopping with the children for their clothes and school supplies, sans Kamalini, on Saturdays.

Kamalini started mumbling to herself, even in the presence of strangers. She would shake her head in agreement or disagreement with herself. Often she would be startled by a simple query like, "Where is my notebook?" She started showing unrealistic concern about the children getting hurt while playing or running, even within the apartment. She would not let them play with the other kids in our building, and she would often shout at them if they accidentally spilled food on the carpet. It was only natural that my daughters wanted me to be around when they were not in school. I would oblige whenever possible.

Kamalini became more and more abrupt in social situations. She had no friends among Canadian or Indian ladies; as far as I knew, it was not in her nature to nurture and cultivate friendships. Indian families—there were seven of them in the apartment complex—declined our invitations for supper and family get-togethers.

In October 1973 we began the construction of our new custom-built home. We spent many Saturday afternoons shopping for paint, light fixtures, carpet, and furniture for the new house. The children enjoyed choosing things for their bedrooms.

One day, we were looking for light fixtures for the bedrooms. Raju and Varsha decided on the light fixtures with Disney characters. There were exactly two available in the store—one had a single lamp and the other had twin lamps. Both wanted the one with the twin lamps. Kamalini was upset with the conversation. She turned to me and said, "Why are you using black magic and causing the conflict between the two?" I ignored her comment without saying a word.

I had an idea to resolve the conflict. "Whoever takes the smallest bedroom will have the first choice." Varsha agreed to go for the smallest bedroom and claimed the twin lamps. Raju was happy to settle for the bigger bedroom. I was pleased with the amicable negotiations between Raju and Varsha.

The following Saturday we all went to choose carpet. Sulabha, Varsha, and Raju unanimously decided on a forest green colour for their bedrooms. This automatically determined the colour of the carpet to be installed throughout the house. To match the carpet, we ordered light emerald green paint for the walls.

I expected Kamalini to be involved in the selection of kitchen cabinets, stove, refrigerator and dishwasher. But she showed no interest.

I did not know whom to approach for help. Since this was not a physical problem, a physician, I thought, would be of no help. Around this time a friend, G.P. Patil, whom we called GP, was visiting the University of Calgary to collaborate on a research project in statistics. After discussing his work, I confided in him about Kamalini's behaviour. GP's face became serious; he looked concerned.

"She needs to be seen by a psychiatrist," he caringly advised me.

I was ignorant. "Psychiatrist? What would he do?"

"A psychological evaluation through an interview," GP explained.

"Kamalini doesn't speak English."

GP thought for a moment, sipping his coffee. "I know a psychiatrist in New York who speaks Marathi."

"New York? It will be too expensive."

"It will be worth it though; it will help you figure out what's happened to Kamalini."

GP gave me the contact information for Dr. Kishore Saraf, and I mailed him a letter requesting an appointment. He responded immediately, and gave Kamalini an appointment for December 27, 1973 at five o'clock in the afternoon. He requested a detailed note on her present symptoms, her family background, and past history of psychological illness and treatment, if any. I prepared a five-page document with the requested information and mailed it to Dr. Saraf.

We started getting ready for the New York trip. The travel costs for five of us were a major concern. The oil-exporting Arab countries, led by Saudi Arabia, had declared an oil embargo after the October 1973 Arab-Israeli war. The airlines had cancelled many flights and available flights were expensive. Kamalini's mental health was my priority and so, in spite of the cost factor, we booked our flights to leave for New York on December 26. Kamalini and I flew with all three children to New York. Kamalini raised no objections, though she was quiet during the entire five-hour flight. It being Boxing Day, the plane was not crowded. Varsha and Sulabha were happy to get window seats.

On December 27 we checked in at the Holiday Inn nearest to the Hillside Hospital in Glen Oaks, where Dr. Saraf's office was. Around four-fifteen we hired a taxi to go to the hospital. It was a half-hour journey from our hotel through the crazy New York traffic. Kamalini and the children sat quietly in the back seat, Kamalini in the centre holding Raju in her lap and Varsha and Sulabha pressed up against the windows on either side enjoying the storefront Christmas decorations. I was in the passenger seat, absorbed in my thoughts. Would Dr. Saraf find a solution to Kamalini's problem? Just before five o'clock, the taxi pulled up in front of the Hillside Hospital. I paid the fare to the driver and got out to open the door for Kamalini and the children. We all walked to the elevators. I picked up Raju and the girls held Kamalini's hand. Dr. Saraf's office was on the fourth floor.

After we waited about ten minutes, Dr. Saraf called me in. Flipping through my report, he said, "Your notes are pretty exhaustive. Would you like to add anything more?"

I summarized Kamalini's behaviour in more detail—the way she had called the police to our apartment, trashed valuable things down the garbage chute, and visited the library in search of an imaginary magazine.

Dr. Saraf looked at me soberly. "These are definitely signs of mental illness," he said.

Ready with the background information, he walked with me to the waiting room and invited Kamalini in for an interview. I stayed behind in the waiting room looking after the children. Varsha was playing with Raju in a kids' corner full of toys. Sulabha had engrossed herself in reading a children's story book. I was feeling restless. A painting on the wall in front of me drew my attention. It showed in the foreground a series of reeds in a field and the setting sun in the background, which gave a depth to the field. While I was engrossed in watching the painting, Kamalini came out of the consulting room followed by Dr. Saraf. He invited me back in to discuss his interview with Kamalini. I asked Kamalini to look after the children, who were still entertaining themselves.

"Kamalini is suffering from schizophrenia," Dr. Saraf said with serious look on his face.

"I've never heard that word." I hesitated. "What does it mean?"

"It's a mental illness resulting from a biochemical imbalance in the brain that causes the patient to behave irrationally."

"Is there a cure?"

"Schizophrenia can't be cured, but can be treated and managed."

"I don't understand."

"It's like diabetes," Dr. Saraf explained patiently. "The cause of diabetes is an insulin imbalance in the pancreas. You can't cure diabetes, but you can control it by managing the insulin level."

"How do you control schizophrenia?"

"We prescribe antipsychotic drugs," Dr. Saraf pulled a prescription pad towards him. "They restore the chemical balance in the brain, but the dose needs regular monitoring. I'm prescribing a hundred milligrams of Thorazine. Contact a psychiatrist in Calgary for monitoring. I'll write a note for him." Dr. Saraf wrote a note on his letter pad and handed it to me.

Out in the hallway, Sulabha asked, "Did you tell the doctor that Mom gets angry for no reason?"

"What did the Doctor say?" asked Varsha.

I looked at Kamalini, who didn't seem to have heard. "Mom suffers from an illness of mind; it's why she acts strange."

"Is there a medicine for the illness?" asked Sulabha, skipping a little to keep up with me.

"Yes, he prescribed a medicine. Mom will have to take it regularly every day."

"It will be nice if Mom stops getting angry," Varsha said, looking up at me.

"Mom's angry because she's sick," I tried to explain. "The medicine will help."

Three years old Raju had no comments. He was too young to understand his mother's illness.

On the way back to the hotel I purchased the prescription from a nearby pharmacy. Kamalini had her first dose the same evening. She was surprisingly cooperative and didn't complain about having to take medication. The next morning while we were having breakfast, Raju spilled his milk. I thought Kamalini would get angry, but she didn't. She quietly wiped first his shirt and then the hotel carpet. I knew that this change in Kamalini's behaviour would not last long without continuous medication. But it raised my hopes that Kamalini's delusions would become the thing of the past.

After returning to Calgary, I searched the yellow pages for a psychiatrist. There weren't many. The listing for Dr. Kazi Islam attracted my attention since it indicated some connection with India. Though I learned more about the mechanism later, it was already clear that ethnic and cultural dynamics played a role in Kamalini's hallucinations. This is true of schizophrenia patients in general; the hallucination of a Christian patient may involve Jesus whereas the hallucination of a Hindu patient may connect to Lord Krishna. The cultural proximity of Dr. Islam, I thought, might be helpful in understanding Kamalini's illness.

We went to see him sometime in the middle of January 1974. I handed him the note from Dr. Saraf and briefed him about our New York visit. Instead of Thorazine, he prescribed ten milligrams of Stelazine, another antipsychotic drug. To control the Parkinson's-like side effects of Stelazine, he prescribed ten milligrams of Kemadrin. Kamalini was to take both pills every night before going to bed.

The combination of the two drugs was effective, but only for a few months. Then we were back to square one. She started spending a disproportionate amount of time doing daily chores. She would leave the tap running for minutes at a time to wash a single utensil. When friends came over to visit, she would not come out of our bedroom. Instead of having meals together with the family, she would enter the kitchen after we had all finished and eat by herself—some cereal with milk or a piece of toast.

She perceived me as an enemy who created all her problems. She accused me of acquiring supernatural powers through black magic and using them to harm her and the children. She went back to using obscene words in Marathi. None of this was easy to stomach. Inside I would be enraged, but I would control myself. I would avoid screaming at her. I knew rational argument was futile. I could only try to remember that Kamalini would not say such horrible things if she were not mentally ill.

Though the winter season was not yet over, it was a warm, sunny Saturday in February. There had been light snow the day before, but the weather changed, becoming beautiful overnight. I announced, "Let's go to see the construction site of our new home." The children were excited. They started getting ready, putting on their shoes and winter jackets. Kamalini was sitting at the kitchen table. I went to her and asked, "Aren't you coming?"

Avoiding looking at me, Kamalini said, "No, I don't feel like it."

Varsha, all set to go, came to us and pleaded, "Come on, Mom! Here's your parka." Kamalini reluctantly took the jacket from Varsha and agreed to join us.

We arrived at the construction site. The drywall was in place, ready to be painted. The contractor was just waiting for us to let him know our decision about the type and colour of carpet. It was a mere matter of a few weeks before the house would be ready.

On our way home, the children were talking amongst themselves about how their bedrooms would look after painting the walls. Kamalini was quiet, aloof and somber; she neither participated in children's discussion nor commented on the construction. What was going through her mind? Was she engrossed in her delusion about my having supernatural powers? I was feeling depressed. I stopped the car by the side of the road on top of a hill.

"What's wrong?" Kamalini asked.

"Why are we building a new home?"

Kamalini's face was blank. She said, "I don't know."

"There is neither peace nor harmony between us," I said. "What is the point in living such a harrowing life?"

"I don't know," Kamalini repeated.

"Why don't I drive over the hill, crash the car, and end the misery for all of us?" I found myself giving voice to the thoughts that were rushing through my mind.

"Please don't!" Kamalini was visibly panicked.

The children did not know what was happening. They started crying. I sat silently in the car looking at the blank expression on Kamalini's face. It took me some time to calm down. Finally, I consoled the children, "Sorry, I didn't mean to quarrel with Mom. I want you to be happy." I started the car. "Let's go to McDonald's for a quick snack?"

2

VOICES IN THE DARK

In April 1974 I communicated to Dr. Islam that the medicines were not effective any more. I expected him to try different medicines and eventually find the one that would work. Instead he suggested, "Let's try electroconvulsive therapy, ECT."

I was immediately on my guard. "You mean shock treatment?"

"Kamalini will not experience any shock," Dr. Islam assured me.

"What do you mean?"

"She will be administered a short-acting anesthesia so that she won't feel the shock."

"What about the side effects?" I asked anxiously.

"Short term memory loss is the primary side effect, but it only lasts a few hours."

Kamalini was sitting beside me, listening to the conversation without asking questions. I asked her if she was comfortable with the procedure. She quietly agreed and signed the consent form. When she started having ECT sessions a few days later, the treatment seemed to work, but only for a few weeks.

Construction work on our new home finished at the end of April. On May 2, we moved from the two-bedroom apartment into our dream home. The children were delighted to have their own bedrooms, and I had a spacious study exclusively for my use, bookshelves to properly organize my library, a place to prepare lectures, to work on research and to carry on my social work. In the family room we set up a big TV for children to watch their favourite cartoons—*Bugs Bunny and Roadrunner* and *The Flintstones*. Kamalini had a spacious walk-in closet in the master bedroom to hang her saris.

Raju found a new friend, Warren Armstrong, who was in his kindergarten class and lived across the street. Raju and Warren became best friends. They walked to and from school together. They played together. During winter months, I would pick up Raju and Warren after school. On such occasions, without fail, Warren would sweetly say, "Thank you, Mr. Wani."

Warren's parents, Roy and Luccia, had three children and they treated Raju like another member of the family. Luccia was a full-time mother. Roy was an optometrist and had a large extended family in Calgary whom the Armstrongs often visited, taking Raju along with them. I am not a sports fan and I never took Raju to hockey or football games, but Roy would always take Raju along with Warren to minor league tournaments and sometimes even to see the Stampeders games at McMahon Stadium. Going to the movies was another family activity that Raju would always be involved in. My daughters were not so lucky. They did make new friends, but they did not bond like Raju and Warren.

When we moved into our new home, Kamalini was still receiving ECT treatment and the treatment was working. She attended to cooking, cleaning and similar other household chores. But she lacked interest in any other activities for her own enjoyment. She pursued her only hobby of studying the weekly sales flyers, clipping coupons and finding bargains. But this state of relative normalcy did not last for long, since ECT was not effective any more. Her oral medications were stopped prior to ECT treatment since they were not having any effect. Kamalini was suddenly without any treatment.

Meanwhile, Dr. Islam advised us to go for family counselling and arranged an appointment with Lucille, a counsellor at the Foothills Hospital. That same evening I brought up the topic at the dinner table. "Mom's doctor has advised us to go for family counselling to help her. We all have to attend."

"I don't need it. I won't come!" Sulabha vehemently banged the table.

"We all have to help Mom. The counsellor won't be able to help if you don't join."

"I don't care," Sulabha said.

"How can you say that?" I asked in frustration.

"Mom isn't sick! It's just your imagination."

I was so taken aback by Sulabha's statement I could not continue the conversation.

Without Sulabha, we all attended the first counselling meeting the following week.

Lucille noticed her absence immediately. "How come Sulabha is not here?"

I informed her of the conversation at the dinner table.

"Counselling won't help without the participation of the entire family," Lucille said shaking her head.

"Is there an alternative?" I asked.

"There is a program for immigrant women at the YWCA that might help Kamalini. The counsellor turned to her.

"Kamalini, would you like to join? You'll meet lots of newcomers to Canada. You'll make new friends. I think you'll enjoy the weekly meetings."

Looking at me, Kamalini said, "I don't mind if my husband would take me there."

"It shouldn't be a problem. I'll find a way," I said.

I called Uma Thakor, the program coordinator at the YWCA. Uma not only encouraged Kamalini to attend, but also arranged transportation for her. Kamalini met women who were new to Canada. She enjoyed their company, and every week she looked forward to attending the next session. Kamalini finally had an opportunity to come out of her loneliness. She made friends with Sunita, an elderly lady from India who drove her to the meetings. Unfortunately, participation in the program was limited to four months. Thereafter, Kamalini did not take any initiative to keep in touch with Sunita or her other new friends and went back into her shell. She would stay in bed all day, not bothering with cooking, cleaning, or washing.

Kamalini's sleep pattern became erratic. She would be awake most of the night, often standing in a nightgown with her hair down looking into the hallway and loudly shouting, "Why are you hiding? Come out in the open and I will teach you a lesson." Kamalini was seeing someone who wasn't there.

Her encounters often deprived us all of a peaceful sleep. Once that winter, in the middle of the night, I woke up to the front door banging shut and realized that Kamalini was probably walking out of the house without any winter clothing. I hurried down the stairs, threw on my jacket, put on my shoes, and followed her. The snow was knee-deep, and I could feel the biting cold. Kamalini was in danger of frostbite. She was standing in the snow, not even wearing boots, looking back at the house and still talking to the imaginary woman inside. I worried that her impassioned argument with the phantom would wake up the neighbourhood. "Please be quiet," I begged her. Without saying a word she started walking back to the house. I opened the door and she came in. She did not resume her conversation with the imaginary person, and both of us went back to sleep.

This happened in December 1974. We wanted to book an appointment with Dr. Islam the next day, but he could not accommodate our request. He suggested we go to the emergency room at the closest hospital. We followed his advice. The psychiatrist on duty interviewed Kamalini and me separately, and then called both of us in for a joint meeting. I do not know what transpired in his interview with Kamalini. Whatever she said to him, the psychiatrist concluded that the problem was our marriage. When both of us were seated in his office he announced, "You should seek a divorce."

I was stunned by the cold, calm advice. His solution was, indeed, simple. I thought about the consequences. Would it really make me happy? Varsha was ten, Sulabha was eight, and Raju was barely four. Kamalini was helpless and needed assistance and care. His "simple" solution meant the breakup of my family. I could not accept the advice of the psychiatrist.

This turmoil developed when I was thirty-seven and Kamalini was thirty. Until schizophrenia began affecting Kamalini in 1972, our marital relations had been normal. Kamalini's illness had a devastating effect on our intimacy. She was not there for me emotionally or physically. I was distressed and helpless. But in spite of our precarious relationship, I was determined to uphold her as a partner for the rest of our lives.

As all of this was happening, Varsha and Sulabha were entering puberty, increasingly needing a motherly figure to help them and to share in their anxieties arising due to the physical and emotional changes they were experiencing at that age. Instead, they were exposed to the severity of Kamalini's mental illness.

Many years later, Sulabha's feelings about her mother came out during a court proceeding: "Even though we have a mother that stays at home, she is not a mother that waits on us hand and foot, has dinner waiting for us, has lunch waiting for us," she said. "We can't understand her sickness; we don't talk to her; we communicate with our father for everything. I never go to our mother and talk about what is going on in my life."

Our routine at home was in total disarray. Kamalini had stopped cooking. Regular meals were out of question. I was not a good cook, and the children never liked the food I prepared for them. Their choices were limited: for lunch as well as dinner, I routinely served a variety of sandwiches made with apple slices, banana slices, cucumber slices, grilled cheese, baloney, and so on. Alternately, they ate microwave dinners or junk food—chips, ice cream, and fries—purchased from the grocery store. It was fortunate that Calgary had a wide variety of Indian snack shops, because my own meals consisted mainly of ready-made Indian snacks such as samosas, Bombay mix with spicy dried ingredients, jalebi, and a variety of sweets.

Raj and Uma Bishnoi, a couple who shared my interest in Indian classical music, came to know about Kamalini being unwell. One evening the Bishnoi couple dropped in to see us. They had brought a meal for us—rice, curries and chapattis—which they set out on the coffee table. Kamalini had been lying down on the sofa; she sat up without acknowledging them, much less thanking them for the food. Raj and Uma in vain tried to talk to Kamalini. Once the children had finished their supper and had gone to their rooms upstairs, we got into a discussion about the vocal concert that had taken place a week before.

After they left, Kamalini lost her temper. "Why did they bring food? I didn't ask them to." I took her outburst in stride, since I had learned that the normal harmony between thought, emotion and behaviour—the three important components of personality—gets disjointed in the case of schizophrenia patients.

The next day I visited the Bishnois and apologized for what had happened. Raj invited me in for a cup of tea. He understandingly said, "There's no need to apologize. We understand your predicament."

––––––––––

I had realized long before, even before Kamalini began exhibiting schizophrenia symptoms, that she just wanted to stay home. Mothers of other children volunteered in the library, in the classrooms, during field trips. Kamalini never attended parent-teacher interviews or took an interest in any of these other activities. She had always been shy and nervous when it came to meeting people. Most of the time, she avoided accompanying me to parties or office events. However, I had to maintain contact with my colleagues and I attended such events without Kamalini. I had dreaded answering the inevitable questions that always came up in these situations about Kamalini's absence, usually offering the excuse that Kamalini wasn't feeling well, that we couldn't get a babysitter, or that we had unexpected house guests. After the diagnosis of schizophrenia, there was no need for any of these excuses. I answered frankly, "Kamalini suffers from schizophrenia and avoids meeting people."

––––––––––

Kamalini was off medication for five years. We lost contact with Dr. Islam and went in search of another psychiatrist who could look into Kamalini's schizophrenia with a fresh perspective, but this was an uphill battle. In the 1970s, Calgary had fewer than half the number of psychiatrists needed to adequately serve the population.

When nothing works and one gets frustrated, one hopes for a miracle. Remaining rational is easier said than done. Neither oral medication nor ECT was effective in controlling Kamalini's schizophrenia. Confounded by the dilemma, I hoped a holy man would help me. As a founding member of the Vedanta Society in Calgary, I came in touch with many monks from the Ramkrishna Mission. Before being initiated into the order, these monks undergo deep spiritual training for years whereby they are supposed to have conquered six enemies which impede the liberation (moksha) of a human being from the cycle of births and deaths. These enemies are sex (kam), anger (krodh), greed (lobh), temptation (moh), arrogance (mad) and jealousy (matsar). It seemed obvious that monks who had completed their training were superior human beings.

I described my problem to two of them during one of their Calgary visits. One of them, Swami Shraddhanand from the Sacramento Vedanta Center, did not give me any false hope. "Monks do not have special powers to cure illness. Never believe it if someone tells you otherwise. Monks may be spiritually at a higher level than a man on the street, but they are still human beings."

"I am devastated," I said. "I don't know what to do."

He tried to console me. "Seek medical help, and keep your cool. Sooner or later, things will improve."

Meanwhile, I had to leave the house only for assigned teaching hours, regular posted office hours, and occasional departmental meetings, which were all scheduled between nine and eleven in the morning and between one and three in the afternoon. I could take care of the other aspects of my work, such as lecture preparation and research, at any time and place. The university was less than five kilometres away from the house. I could stay home until the children left each morning, come back at noon to have lunch with them, and return to the office and come home again at four just before they arrived back from school.

I always drove to work feeling apprehensive, hoping nothing disastrous would happen while Kamalini was alone at home. During the winter months, Kamalini, who always felt cold, often turned the thermostat in the house up past thirty degrees. Outside, the temperature could be as low as forty degrees below zero. The huge difference between the outside and the inside temperatures twice caused the inside panes of the big picture windows to crack. It was not only very expensive to replace them, but I also had to adjust my office schedule so that I would be home when the window workers showed up. I couldn't do anything except ask Kamalini not to touch the thermostat. Fortunately, she never experimented with the cooking range.

While struggling with Kamalini's mental illness, for five years I had no time to concentrate on the research in statistics that was part of my job. In 1977, however, I got an opportunity to catch up. I was due for a six-month sabbatical which I could devote to research without having to teach.

In order to collaborate with other researchers working in my field of interest, I planned visits to institutions in India and Australia. I considered taking the children along, even though it would interrupt their schooling. They were all in elementary school—Raju in grade one, Sulabha in grade five, and Varsha in grade six. When I hesitantly discussed the situation with my brother Chandrakant in India, he immediately offered to look after the children. I hated the thought of leaving my children for six months, and I knew they would not be happy either. Though they had met their uncle six years back in 1972, it was only for a short while. Raju then was barely a year and a half old, Sulabha was six and Varsha was eight. Moreover, the living conditions in India and Canada were vastly different. But I couldn't escape the fact that I needed time to concentrate on research if I was going to retain my position at the U of C.

I accepted the offer from my brother and he secured admission for the children at an English convent school in Dhule, my hometown.

Before I began my research, we all traveled to Dhule to visit the school and meet the teachers. I briefed them about the children's education in Canada. A language course in Hindi, the national language of India, was compulsory according to the Indian education system. Since the children were going to be in the school only for a semester, I made a request to the Mother Superior to exempt them from this course. She was very willing to accommodate my request. Chandrakant wanted Kamalini to stay with the children to make the transition smoother. It was a good idea, though I cautioned him that Kamalini's behaviour was unpredictable and might make things more difficult. I told him how she got upset when the Bishnois brought food for us. Not fully understanding the nature of her illness, he believed that the change in environment would help her. He talked to Kamalini and she agreed to stay in Dhule while I went to Mumbai.

I intended to spend few weeks at the Tata Institute of Fundamental Research to collaborate with Dr. Vasant Tikekar, one of my friends from college days, who happened to be at the institute at that time. Barely a week had passed after arriving at the institute when I received a telegram from my brother: "Return to Dhule immediately." I caught the evening train. I could not sleep the whole night thinking about the possible reasons for the telegram. Was Sulabha creating problems? Was one of the children severely ill? Had Kamalini done something so strange that my brother had to summon me back? The train arrived in Dhule around eight o'clock in the morning. I waved down an auto rickshaw and gave the driver dressed in khaki uniform directions to my brother's house. When I jumped out of the rickshaw, I saw my brother sitting in a cane chair on the veranda, anxiously waiting for me.

"What happened?" I asked.

"I can't deal with Kamalini."

I looked past Chandrakant, trying to see into the house. "What's wrong?"

"She's perpetually angry and irritable. It's starting to affect the children."

"Are you having problems with the children?"

"No, except for Sulabha's non-cooperation. Instead of persuading Sulabha to go to school, Kamalini encourages her to stay home. Varsha and Raju have a set routine—school, homework and playing with their cousins. Sulabha just sits around."

"Is there a psychiatrist in Dhule?"

Chandrakant was puzzled. "What's a psychiatrist? I never heard of one in Dhule," he said.

"I will take Kamalini with me. Are you still willing to look after the children?"

"Sure, they're happy. My children, Munnie, Chunnie and Pappu, are enjoying having them here."

The next day, Kamalini and I left for Bangalore. I was planning to spend two months there at the Indian Institute of Science collaborating with Dr. Tikekar, who had since returned from the Tata Institute to his home base. Without the responsibility of children and not having to do any house work, the situation was less stressful for Kamalini.

My next stop was at Monash University in Australia. Dr. Geoffrey Watterson from Monash had published a paper very closely related to my research area—the distribution of species of moths and butterflies. Before leaving for Australia, Kamalini and I visited Dhule to see our children.

Raju had developed an attachment to my brother. He needed his uncle to be around for every little thing—meals, baths, and every other routine activity. He would refuse to take a bus to go to school, insisting that his uncle personally drop him off at the school on his motorcycle. He would keep my brother awake late into the night so that he could help him complete his homework.

Raju was particular and punctual about his homework. Apparently, he was always delightful in dealing with his teachers and Mother Superior. No wonder he became a favourite with them. When they learned he had developed an illness, they all came to visit him, bringing along balloons and toys.

Varsha was happy in Dhule, even happy-go-lucky. She suffered from a stomach ache on and off but attended school regularly. She was very cooperative and easily got along with everyone. She found a good friend, Rukhsana Godrej, at the school who, unlike other local children, was from a cosmopolitan family who had moved from Mumbai to Dhule. After Varsha returned to Canada, the two kept in touch with each other for several decades. Varsha was so friendly with her teachers that during our brief stay she invited all of them to go to a movie with all of us.

Twelve-year old Sulabha was not happy. I tried to convince her that she should look at the India visit as a learning experience, an opportunity to know another country that very few children get. She was not convinced. She often refused to go to school. She suffered from allergies and eczema but declined to take medication and was uncooperative with the doctor. She vented her unhappiness through arrogance and swearing and created lots of stress for my brother.

All three children came with my brother and his family to see us off at the railway station. Sulabha was in tears and gave me a hug before we boarded the train. I was very touched by her affection. Raju and Varsha cheerfully waved to us as the train pulled out of the station.

Dr. Watterson came to receive us at the Melbourne airport and drove us to the Monash campus where he had arranged our accommodation in a guest apartment, which Kamalini was delighted with. It was a stress-free environment for Kamalini.

Right after we left for Australia, Raju developed a fever and was sick for many weeks. As Chandrakant told me later, he lost weight and became very weak. My father was very concerned. He wanted Chandrakant to call me immediately to inform us about Raju's health. However, Chandrakant did not want the worry to distract me. He sought the opinion of the pediatrician, and on her advice decided not to inform me.

Sulabha continued to cause problems. In one of his letters to me Chandrakant wrote, "We are all scared of her unpredictable behaviour. She is a terror for all of us." Varsha and Raju enjoyed their school and had developed a strong liking for their uncle. In spite of Sulabha's rude behaviour, my brother was firm in seeing through his promise to me.

Our situation on sabbatical was less stressful for Kamalini, and her peace of mind in turn helped me to concentrate on research. The children missed me very much, even though I knew Chandrakant and his wife Lata were caring for them with love and affection. In every letter my brother wrote to me, Raju added a sentence in his own handwriting: "I want my daddy now!"

When Kamalini and I returned from Australia in early December, we all went on a sightseeing tour of North India. The children enjoyed seeing the Taj Mahal, Agra Fort, Jama Masjid and other tourist attractions in Delhi and Agra, the famous Hawa Mahal and Amber Fort in Jaipur, also known as the pink city. We could never see such places in Canada. The Amber Fort entrance could be reached by walking up the hill, driving up in a car, or taking a lurching elephant ride. The children unanimously opted for the elephant ride. Excited by the idea of riding such a great beast, they were ready to leave home by eight o'clock in the morning. Our host, Kamalini, and I went up by car and waited for the children. Amber Fort is like something out of a fairy tale—breathtaking palaces, halls, gardens, and temples set on a hill top overlooking a lake.

On the way down from the fort, Sulabha announced, "I am thirsty. I want water."

"Sorry, in the rush I forgot to bring the bottle of boiled water," our host apologized.

"It'll be less than an hour before we reach home. Can you wait?" I asked.

"No, I'm thirsty, I want water right now!" Sulabha was shouting.

"We can stop at a café for water, but we will not get boiled water."

"Well maybe they'll have Coke or something," Sulabha said in a grouchy voice.

"I'm thirsty too," said Varsha, "but I don't want to get sick from ordinary water. I'll wait until we get back home."

We stopped at the next wayside café. They did not have any bottled drinks. Of course water was available.

"Sulabha, we do not know how safe the water is," I pleaded once again. "We have been careful about only drinking boiled water. Why take a risk? Just wait for half an hour and you will get water from the fridge at home."

"No, I want water right now!" screamed Sulabha at the top of her voice.

I was not surprised with Sulabha's demand. I don't recall any moment when she was cooperative. I gave up in frustration and Sulabha drank the water. Within weeks of our return to Canada, she came down with jaundice.

A few months after I returned from sabbatical, the dean of the Faculty of Science called me to know if I would accept a nomination for the position of the chairman of the Statistics Division. An administrative position such as this would have added heavily to my workload. Kamalini's deteriorating mental health would not permit me to accept such a demanding assignment. I had no choice but to decline the offer.

———————

I wanted Kamalini to see Dr. Islam and again resume treatment for her schizophrenia. She simply refused. I began to think of finding some legal avenue to force her to see a psychiatrist. I learned, however, that there was no recourse unless she was proven to be a threat to herself or others. What kind of system was this? Kamalini was a confirmed patient suffering from mental illness. Why couldn't she be forced to be treated? Why would they expect me to wait until she proved to be a threat? I was helpless.

3

OUT FROM THE DARK

I was driving to work in February 1980 when an announcer on a local radio station said something that caught my attention: "My guest Bill Jefferies is touring Canada to create awareness about schizophrenia." Bill was talking about the nature of schizophrenia, its prevalence, and the problems faced by the caregivers. "The patient doesn't accept his mental illness, and the helpless family is traumatized by the patient's bizarre behaviour," he explained. His statements struck a chord. "How true," I muttered to myself, "Isn't this what I'm going through right now?" Bill concluded by inviting anyone interested to a public meeting on Wednesday, March 5.

Sixteen people showed up for the meeting. Bill was calm without exhibiting the aura of a man bringing schizophrenia out of the closet. He was dressed very simply with a jacket but no tie. He was accompanied by his wife, Dorothy, and his son, David. One by one, the attendees introduced themselves and told their personal stories. We were all startled when a woman in her early sixties, neatly dressed in a light blue sweater, commented, "I wish my son had cancer instead of schizophrenia." She continued in a quavering tone, "If he had cancer, our friends and family would sympathize with us. How can I tell them about schizophrenia?

They won't even understand what that means. What kind of future will he have?"

There was stunned silence. The word 'cancer' sends shivers down any spine. It occurred to me that parents can only cope with cancer because the patient understands what cancer is, and cooperates in treatment. Schizophrenia patients cannot understand or accept their illness. Bill broke the silence, "We're all in the same boat. I have three family members facing this debilitating illness—two brothers and a son. I know how mental health professionals treat families and how they often blame the families." He continued, "Even though no other illness requires more ongoing support from families and friends than schizophrenia, the research funding for mental illnesses is insignificant compared to the funding provided for most physical illnesses.

"How do we deal with this situation?" Pointing his finger at the audience, Bill challenged us. "You can make the difference. Let's come together and help ourselves. We need a united voice to present our case at public forums and to government departments. Come forward. Let's form a self-help group here in Calgary."

A man whose son was a schizophrenia patient, and who had already introduced himself as the president of one of the units of the Canadian Union of Public Employees in Calgary, volunteered to act as the president of the group. His wife announced that she would be the secretary. The audience was surprised by the couple's offer; they looked sceptical. I said to Bill, "I am not aspiring to any position, but I'll help with completing the formalities necessary to register a self-help group in Calgary."

After the meeting, Bill approached me and asked if we could meet to discuss the process of registering the Alberta chapter. He was staying with his son David, an architect, in Calgary. The next day, I settled into a chair in David's living room, and over a cup of coffee Bill inquired about Kamalini's condition and told me more about his own background. In devastating situations, it is always easier to find a shoulder to cry on than to accept the challenge courageously and help others suffering the same plight. Bill, however, had taken early retirement from his position as a school principal after a twenty-five-year teaching career to devote himself to creating awareness about schizophrenia and to bringing patients' families together. Of his two brothers who had schizophrenia, one was a former physician who had lived in an asylum until his death.

In February, Bill told me, he had held a meeting in Edmonton attended by nine people, including Mary Fitzgerald, whose son had schizophrenia. She was also interested in forming a self-help group. Bill recommended we form a provincial group rather than two different chapters in two cities and gave me Mary's phone number.

Before I got a chance to phone Mary, she phoned me, "When can we meet to organize an Alberta chapter of Friends of Schizophrenics?" Mary's enthusiasm was evident in her voice.

"Well, the Calgary group is meeting tomorrow to discuss the objects and the by-laws," I said. "Are you free to join us?"

Mary flew into Calgary the next day. The meeting was held in the evening in a classroom at the University. Seven people showed up, including David Jefferies. At the meeting, Mary recalled Bill's talk on CBC radio. "I was sitting at home taking notes and splattering the desktop with tears of relief," she said. All of us in the meeting were touched by Mary's comments. I thanked Mary for coming all the way to Calgary to attend the meeting. Mary attended two more meetings, spending a sizeable amount of her own money to pay for the airline tickets. By mid-April, the first draft of incorporation documents was ready for circulation to everyone who'd attended the initial meetings in Calgary and Edmonton.

———

Kamalini's deteriorating mental health began to affect her physical health, and I had to place the formation of the self-help group on the back burner. She slouched on the living room sofa day and night. I offered to make tea for her and tried to bring her breakfast in the mornings, but without any response, she always turned her face the other way. Fortunately, I had great support from Raju, though he was only nine. He took it upon himself to take care of his mother. Every morning, before leaving for school, Raju served her chocolate chip cookies and a glass of milk. He did the same when he came home for lunch at noon.

In fact, Kamalini was eating nothing except cookies and milk. She became weak and pale and needed to be seen immediately by a psychiatrist. On May 1, 1980, I called Dr. Islam and booked an appointment. I asked Kamalini to join me, but she refused. I had no choice but to go alone.

"This is serious," Dr. Islam said. "Life threatening, in fact. We need to have her admitted as soon as possible."

"She won't agree."

"You have to try." Dr. Islam tried to encourage me.

"What if she doesn't?"

"In that case, I'll arrange for two social workers to visit your home. They'll try to persuade her to come to the hospital. If they fail, then I'll have to take the legal route."

As expected, my conversation with Kamalini was fruitless. The very next day Dr. Islam sent two social workers to our house. They approached Kamalini, who was lying on the living room sofa. Kamalini didn't want to acknowledge their presence. One of them said to her, "Kamalini, you are not well. You need treatment at the hospital."

"I don't need any treatment! Take my husband to the hospital. He is the one who needs treatment," Kamalini retorted.

"You look frail and weak." The social worker gently took Kamalini's arm. "Whether you like it or not, we are taking you to the hospital."

Kamalini grudgingly agreed to go with them. While getting into their car, she turned to me. "May God punish you for what you are doing to me. You will go to Hell. God will never forgive you."

I followed the social workers to the hospital. With the help of the hospital staff, they had Kamalini admitted. A nurse took her to the designated ward. The doctor on call ordered blood tests and asked me to come to the hospital the next day to meet with him and discuss the results of the tests. The next day, we walked together to Kamalini's ward.

"Kamalini's hemoglobin count is down to 4.6." The physician looked concerned. "A normal hemoglobin count is at least 13. Her life is in danger."

"What can we do?" I asked.

He shrugged. "A blood transfusion is probably our best bet."

"I won't accept that," protested Kamalini, who was listening to the conversation. "I won't accept that. Why should I let someone else's blood into my body?"

I tried to persuade her. "Don't you want to get well? We have to accept the advice of the doctor."

"Don't talk to me." Kamalini glared. "You're the cause of my problem."

I turned to the physician and asked, "What's the alternative?"

"I can prescribe various vitamins," he said. "They'll work, but the process will be slow. It will take a few months for her hemoglobin level to return to normal."

"Will Kamalini have to stay in the hospital?"

"No, but she will have to be seen by a psychiatrist." He looked at me, and then clapped me on the shoulder. "Think about what you feel you should do and then we can decide on a course of action."

Kamalini firmly refused blood transfusion, though she seemed more than willing to take vitamin pills. She was kept in the hospital for three weeks, until the physician was satisfied with the progress of her recovery. After coming home, she continued taking her prescribed supplements. As the doctor predicted, in about four months, her hemoglobin count was normal again.

_____

Kamalini's fear of a transfusion turned out to be a blessing in disguise. During those years, the process of screening donated blood was not advanced, and more than one thousand Canadians who received blood donations during the 1970s were infected with HIV; at least another twenty thousand more contracted hepatitis C. This resulted in a class-action lawsuit, and the tainted blood scandal was a legal issue for many decades.

_____

Sayali, an old family friend from India, visited us in June that year. She was vacationing in the Banff and Jasper national parks after attending a conference of journalists in Banff. During a conversation with me one day, she began musing about the reasons for Kamalini's illness.

"Kamalini had been a young housewife when she arrived in Montreal from India. She had very little knowledge of English and had no previous exposure to the Western lifestyle," Sayali said. "I believe that loneliness helped trigger her mental illness."

"I don't agree," I said. "If this was true, her mental illness would have surfaced earlier, not nine years after arriving in Canada. During her first two years in Montreal, Kamalini enjoyed shopping, trampling in the snow, enduring cold weather—all of it."

"Then what triggered it?" Sayali asked.

"I think about that constantly, but I have no answer. However, it all began after our 1972 India trip, which was filled with a chain of unpleasant experiences from beginning to end."

_____

Dr. Peter Roxburgh was the attending psychiatrist when Kamalini was being treated for malnutrition at the Foothills hospital. The day after she was admitted, we met in one of the hospital cafeterias. Peter opened the conversation by asking about my work at the university, but after we'd chatted informally for a few minutes, the subject matter became more serious. "How is the general atmosphere at home?" he asked, sipping black coffee. I related all the events leading up to Kamalini's hospitalization. Peter paused for a minute and in a soft sympathetic voice responded, "I can appreciate what you're going through, and I'd emphasize that you should not consider yourself responsible for what's happened to Kamalini."

"It's a relief to hear you say that. I think the general public assumes that the family and the surrounding environment are the cause of mental illness." Peter shook his head. "That's a myth. There's no scientific evidence. When did Kamalini first receive any treatment for schizophrenia?"

I told him about the Thorazine treatment under Dr. Saraf, later switched to Stelazine combined with Kemadrin by Dr. Islam, and about the ECT treatment, which seemed to work temporarily.

"Should we go back to ECT?" I asked.

"No. I don't treat any of my patients with ECT," Peter responded emphatically.

"Why?"

"It is a controversial treatment. There are no convincing long-term studies. We could try injectable Fluphenazine. Also known as Modecate."

Peter explained, "Modecate is more potent than Thorazine or Stelazine. The main benefit of injected Modecate is its long-acting effect, but the side effects include Parkinson's-like symptoms, such as shaking hands or fingers, which are common to other antipsychotic drugs. Another drug, Cogentin, could control this side effect. Initially, Kamalini would receive a Modecate injection once a week, starting at the maximum suggested dose, which would be slowly reduced along with the frequency of her injections until she comes to a stage of receiving a low dose every three weeks. The exact schedule would depend on how Kamalini responds during each stage of the treatment."

It sounded too promising not to agree to try. I said, "Let's hope this will work. If it does it would be a big relief for the whole family."

Peter made me feel comfortable from that very first meeting and his counselling reassured me that a caregiver needs counselling as much as a patient, if not more. Peter's empathetic attitude was a pleasant surprise—especially after the psychiatrist who suggested Kamalini and I divorce.

While Kamalini was in the hospital, I was helping to plan a concert with Calgary's Raga-Mala Music Society, to be held on Saturday, May 10. Some of the other executive members asked me if the after-concert reception could be held at my home. I'd told them about Kamalini's hospital admission and they promised to look after all the arrangements for food and drinks. I was hesitant. I thought, though, that perhaps Kamalini could come home for the reception and get a break from the drab routine at the hospital. I obtained permission from Dr. Roxburgh to have her released for that evening, and after the concert, I went to the hospital and brought Kamalini home. When we arrived, Kamalini's friend Uma Thakor from the YWCA opened the door.

"Welcome home Kamalini!" Uma beamed.

"I am sorry that I could not make any of the arrangements," Kamalini apologized.

"We all understand, Kamalini. Everything is organized, just relax."

Uma guided us in and introduced Kamalini to the main artists, the well-known Indian flute player Hariprasad Chaurasia and the tabla player Zakir Hussain. Both musicians courteously asked Kamalini about her health.

Uma brought her a plate of food. Kamalini smiled nervously, trying to hold her plate securely, and said to Mr. Chaurasia, who was standing next to her, "I missed an excellent concert. I understand it was sold out."

"The concert is recorded, so you can still listen to it," said Chaurasia gently.

The effects of her medication were obvious. Kamalini was slow in her movements, but she was still making an effort to communicate with the guests. She thanked Uma for the delicious food she had prepared with the help of other members of the society. Since the reception was after the concert, it had started late; by that time the children were in bed, so Kamalini could not interact with them.

As Kamalini's newest treatment progressed, it became clear that the injectable Modecate was working very well. I did not even have to worry about the injection schedule. Kamalini was keeping track of it and reminding me to take her to the clinic to receive her injections.

Under the treatment of Dr. Roxburgh, Kamalini's schizophrenia came under control for the first time since she was undergoing ECT five years before. I was relieved of the worries at home. Kamalini took on the regular household chores and started looking after the children. They were happy to see their mother in a pleasant mood. Instead of eating cold sandwiches every day, the children started enjoying hot meals prepared by Kamalini.

Around the same time, the appointment of a new Head of the Department of Mathematics and Statistics brought changes to my work environment and it became harmonious once again. Suddenly I had some spare time, as well as peace of mind, to devote to the formation of the self-help group. The incorporation documents were signed on July 27, and the

Alberta Friends of Schizophrenics was officially incorporated on July 29 as an organization under the Societies Act of Alberta. (The word "schizophrenics" is often used in offensive way and hence the organization later changed its name to Schizophrenia Society of Alberta [SSA].)

In 1980, Calgary, the fastest growing city in Canada, was facing a severe shortage of psychiatrists. The *Calgary Herald* not only gave wide coverage to the formation of the SSA but also coupled it with an editorial challenging the provincial government to act.

The Calgary chapter of the society held its first public meeting on September 23, 1980, in the Foothills Hospital auditorium. More than sixty people attended, most of them caregivers. Almost everyone enthusiastically entered their names, phone numbers, and addresses in the attendance book, requesting to be added to the mailing list. Today, the SSA has hundreds of members across Alberta, but this was the first time that families of people with schizophrenia had a chance to congregate in a public meeting in Calgary. The guest speaker that night was Dr. Keith Pearce, head of psychiatry at the University of Calgary. At the end of his talk, the audience bombarded him with questions.

"Is there a physical test to detect schizophrenia or susceptibility to it?"

"Unfortunately, no."

"Is electroshock treatment useful?"

"Though it's controversial, it may be useful."

"How can we make a patient realize that they require treatment?"

"There is no easy solution; you need to seek help from a psychiatrist."

"What's the percentage of people in the general population that have schizophrenia?"

"One in a hundred."

Within a year after the registration of the SSA, two families faced the trauma of dealing with the suicides of their beloved sons, men in their early twenties. Both families requested that their relatives and friends make donations to the SSA in lieu of flowers.

Schizophrenia typically strikes young people in their high school years or early twenties, and the teenager coping with the illness may become a subject of fellow students' ridicule, which further aggravates the problem. The ridicule, sometimes, leads to isolation and in the extreme case to suicide. The two suicides within the families of SSA members convinced us to begin creating awareness programs aimed at high school students. Creating awareness within small peer groups is as important as creating awareness in the general populace. Joan Nuckles, who was then the president of the Calgary chapter, and Dr. Sabastian Littman, the head of psychiatry department at the University of Calgary, took the leading roles in this activity. They organized awareness meetings in high schools and impressed upon the students how compassion, understanding, and cooperation from a peer group can make life easier for the person dealing with the illness. Literature and other media sources were scant in those days. To make up for this scarcity, Dr. Littman prepared a short write-up to be distributed to the students.

As time went on, the SSA's provincial board meetings started focusing more on discussion and less on action. Bylaw revisions and the structure of the board became the central issues of concern. The SSA could not afford to rent an office space; hence these meetings were held either at my home in Calgary or at Mary's home in Edmonton. (My residence was the official address of the SSA while I served as a board member.) One such board meeting was held on a Sunday afternoon in Calgary in our living room. All board members—three from Edmonton and three from Calgary—were in attendance. After the discussion on the revision of board structure, I broached my interest in initiating some concrete action. I wanted to use my limited spare time to raise funds for awareness programs. I spoke up. "Let's discuss creating an endowment at the U of C to award scholarships as a way of encouraging medical students to include the subject of mental illness in their studies. As per the policy of the provincial government any amount we shall raise and hand over to the university the government will match that amount on one to one basis."

"The scholarship amount will not even pay for a sandwich," commented a fellow board member, with a certain tone of contempt, without even letting me explain any further details. Rather than get frustrated, I decided to withdraw from the provincial board to devote more time to the Calgary chapter, where my fellow board members were action-oriented. We all decided to initiate a scholarship project. With the encouraging support of the board, I wrote to all the major corporations (mainly oil companies) in Calgary, seeking donations. I even sent a request letter to *the Calgary Herald*, which had given us good publicity during the SSA's early days. The response was surprisingly positive. The donations ranged from fifty to two hundred fifty dollars, with the largest donation coming from the Nova Corporation. We carried out two more rounds of letter campaigns, one in 1984 and the other in 1985, with reasonable success. I used my association with the Raga-Mala Performing Arts of Canada and arranged two dance performances, which raised a few thousand dollars for the scholarship fund, bringing the total to fifteen thousand dollars. We passed the money over to the University of Calgary and the provincial government matched the amount, bringing the total endowment to thirty thousand dollars. Today, the interest on the endowment provides enough income to award an annual scholarship of one thousand dollars to a graduate or post-graduate student whose research pertains to the study of schizophrenia. The Calgary chapter later renamed the scholarship in honour of the late Dr. Sabastian Littman who actively promoted the activities of the SSA.

———————

During the 1980s, pharmaceutical companies kept introducing new drugs to help control schizophrenia, but their research and development of new drugs did not uncover the underlying cause of the illness. We felt the need for sustained research, and hence in 1988, the Calgary chapter began fundraising to create a chair for schizophrenia research at the University of Calgary. We successfully raised more than eight hundred thousand dollars within a span of three years, and the provincial government matched these funds two-to-one. This brought the total endowment to two and a half million dollars. Having received the requisite amount to set up an endowment, the university then set up a committee of experts to search for a deserving candidate to be appointed to occupy the chair for schizophrenia research.

———————

I was offered the position of chairman of the statistics division in 1982. Kamalini's schizophrenia was under control. The children were grown up and did not need as much attention—Varsha in grade twelve was doing well in her studies, Sulabha in grade eleven was having sixteen-year-old jitters wanting to be solely responsible in dealing with her school administration, and Raju in grade six was just enjoying the company of his friend Warren. This atmosphere encouraged me to accept the offer of chairmanship. The position offered me an opportunity to fulfill my dream of initiating an undergraduate degree program in Actuarial Science. (This relatively unknown discipline deals with the financial risks associated with the lives of individuals—life insurance, pensions, and similar other topics.) The program started with seven students, but this number kept rising consistently every year and in 2004 enrolment exceeded two hundred students. Twenty-three years later in 2005, an external review committee of two experts noted: "The number of students in the Actuarial Science program has increased rather dramatically—a very healthy situation. Indeed, this is one of the most impressive accomplishments of the department in recent years."

After many years of hard work, the SSA was well established, with chapters in many cities and towns across Alberta and a membership count in the hundreds. I now began to feel I could do something similar for India, my native land. Bill was my role model. He had taken his mission beyond his small town of Oakville to every province in Canada. I began to wonder if I too could expand my horizons and take the schizophrenia awareness program beyond Canada, across the oceans, to my native land.

4

OUT OF THE NEST

After finishing my final year of high school in 1954, I spent my summer vacation with my cousin, Kashinath, helping him in his general store in the small town of Kopargaon. At the end of May, on my way home from Kopargaon, I decided to take a break, spend a day at the summer camp in Chalisgaon, and meet up with some of my high school buddies who were attending the camp. It was run by a youth association, Rashtra Seva Dal—the National Service Corps, about fifty kilometres from Dhule, my home town.

GP Patil, then a young man in his early twenties, was also visiting the camp. With his simple grey bush shirt, matching trousers, and smiling face, GP impressed me as a friendly person. His eyeglasses made him look like a scholar, and indeed, he was studying for master's degree in statistics at the University of Pune. Just after seven o'clock the next morning, when we had all gathered in the dining room for breakfast, GP rushed up to me waving a newspaper in his hand. "Congratulations, Jagan!"

I was confused. I thought he was teasing me. "What for?"

"Haven't you read the news?"

"What news?"

GP flashed the front-page headline: JAGANNATH WANI ONLY MARATHI-SPEAKING STUDENT ON SSC EXAMINATION MERIT LIST. (SSC is the abbreviation for Secondary School Certificate.)

"I knew I did well, but I didn't expect to be in the top fifteen!" I said in disbelief. About a hundred thousand students wrote the SSC exam every year.

My friends from high school and the other campers gathered around me. "Wow! Nine Gujarati, five Kannada, and only one Marathi! We're proud of you, Jagan," one of them said, patting me on my back.

"Aren't you celebrating? How about some peda?" asked another. (Peda is an Indian sweet made by simmering full-fat milk in an iron pot for several hours, over a medium fire, gradually vaporizing its water content leaving coagulated solids in milk, and then adding sugar and saffron to it.)

"I'll come again to distribute sweets. I have to catch the train to see my parents." I said.

"Leave it to me, Jagan," GP said. "I'll get some peda and distribute it at lunch time. Go catch the train. Your parents must be waiting for you."

GP's spontaneous affection was overwhelming and surprising. We had only known each other for a few hours, but GP seemed like an elder brother who could guide me in ways my family could not—my father had barely completed grade three, and my mother had no formal education. Before I left the camp coordinator said, "You are in league with GP; he also secured a place on the SSC merit list five years ago."

I hurried to the train station and purchased a copy of each of all the newspapers available. Every front page announced the news about the SSC results, prominently displaying the merit list under bold headlines. *Loksatta*, a widely read Marathi newspaper, reported, "No students from Mumbai or Pune on the merit list. Jagannath Wani from Dhule ranked 9th."

The SSC merit list had always been dominated by students from well-known schools in Mumbai and Pune—major cities, each with populations in the hundreds of thousands, and each with a university with many affiliated colleges. Dhule was an obscure small town whose population barely exceeded thirty thousand. Educational activity in the town did not extend beyond a few high schools. Cotton and peanuts were major commercial crops in the surrounding areas and most young people went to work at the ginning plants, separating lint from cotton seeds, or the oil mills, extracting oil from peanuts. A local farmer's son appearing in the SSC merit list was a major event for the whole town.

I boarded the train with all the newspapers in hand. At eight o'clock, the train pulled out of the station. It made a journey of barely fifty-five kilometres in two hours, stopping at half a dozen stations on the way. The monsoon rains had yet to arrive. Though it was still early in the morning, there was no relief from the scorching summer heat shimmering above the semi-desert landscape. The train crossed bridges over many rivers, some small and some large, all dry and lifeless. But the barren land and waterless rivers could not affect my elated mood. I was eager to see my family and share the news with them.

I was thinking about the excitement at home when the train pulled into the station at Dhule. I hurried out of the station and waved down a tanga, a horse-drawn cart with a black canopy. It was the only vehicle in town available for hire in those days. I got into the tanga, the driver, dressed in khaki shorts, a white shirt, and a black cap, shook the reins, and the horse started trotting. The magical sound of its hoof beats, clip-clop, clip-clop, clip-clop, echoed through the streets. Avoiding small children rushing to their schools, the tanga took me through a maze of alleyways that had not changed in decades. After about fifteen minutes we pulled up in front of our house. Nana, my father, was waiting for me. I touched his feet; he patted me on the back. "We were all waiting for you.

To celebrate your grand success I've bought two kilos of peda to distribute amongst your teachers, our relatives, friends, and neighbours." Saying this, he put a piece of peda in my mouth.

I was excited to share the news of my success with Aabaa Deshpande, my favourite high school teacher. Nana accompanied me to his house. It was sweltering. Aabaa, a hefty man with a large belly, was sitting in a cane chair without a shirt, waving a fan in his hand. I touched his feet to show my respect and presented him with a box of sweets. He hugged me and patted me on the back. He waved to my father and me to have seats on the cane sofa in front of his chair.

"Jagannath's performance has been stunning," Aabaa said to Nana. "Where are you going to send him for college?"

"No college, I'm going to get him married," Nana half-joked.

"What? What's the hurry? Marriage is a routine matter. Everyone gets married, but not everyone shines on the merit list," Aabaa said.

"In our community, most boys get married at sixteen. Jagannath is nineteen."

"Jagannath is not one of those boys. Let him complete his college education," Aabaa said, vigorously waving the fan in his hand.

Nana became more serious. "College is an additional expense. I would rather get him into farming."

"That's your perspective. Why don't you let him decide? Even you'll admit that farming isn't the only choice."

"We've been farming for generations," Nana retorted. "And Jagannath is the eldest son. At my age, I need some help."

"I understand, but look at it another way. Being a bright student, Jagannath will make a name for himself outside of the farming world and make you proud through his achievements."

"Can I express an opinion?" I asked Nana.

"What is it?" Nana gave me a puzzled look.

"I'd like to continue my education." My stomach was churning. I looked at my father. "Just because we've been farming for generations doesn't mean it's the best career for me."

"Sending Jagannath to a college will squeeze your budget, but in the end, Jagannath will be a happier person," Aabaa said.

"Since elementary school, I've been getting scholarships, and you never had to pay my tuition fees," I said to Nana. "I should be getting scholarships in college too. I won't be a financial burden."

"Let me think," Nana continued, looking at Aabaa. "I shall have to seriously consider the financial implications."

After the conversation Nana and I got up to leave. I looked back gratefully at Aabaa, who got up from his chair and accompanied us to the door.

The conversation with Aabaa had a profound effect on Nana. He decided to let me go to college. He wanted me to apply to the nearest college, located about thirty kilometres west of Dhule. I wrote a letter to GP seeking his advice. He wrote back, "Though it will be less expensive to study at a nearby college, the rural environment will not provide you with much opportunity for personal development. I suggest you apply to Fergusson College in Pune. Not only students from different parts of India but also from abroad come to Fergusson to study."

In the evening Nana returned home from the farm. I showed him the letter and told him about GP and his affection for me. Nana could not afford to send me to Fergusson College. Fortunately, my cousin Kashinath happened to be visiting us. Overhearing our conversation, he interrupted, "Why worry about expenses? Getting educated at a renowned college is important. I shall take care of all the expenses; Jagannath can pay me back after he starts earning a living with his degree."

I was delighted. Nana accepted the unexpected offer from my cousin and I enrolled at Fergusson College in Pune.

During the previous year, while GP had been serving as a dormitory superintendent at the college, he established an organization called Dnyana Sadhana ("pursuit of knowledge") for the dorm residents. The organization's purpose was to broaden the outlook of its members by providing opportunities to meet eminent personalities from time to time, have discussions, and receive guidance to further their career goals. As soon as I arrived, GP started pestering me to get involved in the group. Coming from a small town and trying to adjust to the environment at a cosmopolitan college, I was hesitant. One evening GP dropped in and stayed overnight with me. During the course of our long conversation, he said to me, "Scholastic achievement alone is not enough to be successful in life."

"What do you mean?" I asked.

"Interpersonal skills are equally important."

"Joining Dnyana Sadhana means participating in group discussions. I'm too nervous," I said.

Smiling while looking at me, GP said, "Sooner or later you have to get over it. Not only should you be a member, you should also join the executive committee."

"What?"

In the end, I did join the executive committee.

The organization's annual gathering in April was the last function of the year. I had to arrange a sports activity jointly with another executive committee member, Ms. Usha Gokhale. I had never had a conversation with a woman my own age. In the small-town schools I attended there had been no girls; boys and girls were segregated right from the elementary level. Coeducation started only in the first year of college.

I nervously walked to the ladies' dorm, which was on the opposite end of the campus. The dorms of the boys and the girls were separated by the college buildings in between them. Unlike the boys' dorm, the girls' dorm was secured with a fence. I was confused and very uncomfortable. I had no idea how I was going to start my first conversation with a girl. A watchman with gruff face was standing at the compound gate. I approached him and said, "I am Jagannath Wani. Please let Ms. Gokhale know that I would like to meet her. It's about the Dnyana Sadhana function."

"There are three Gokhales. Do you know the first name?" He had a harsh voice that made me even more nervous.

"Usha," I said.

The watchman disappeared into the building and returned. I had a few minutes to compose myself before Usha arrived at the gate. She was not tall, maybe five feet two, with fair skin. Her light brown sari looked good on her. I mustered all my courage and said, "We have to plan a few games for the Dnyana Sadhana's annual gathering."

"Have you thought of any?" she asked.

"Musical Chairs?"

She laughed, twisting the end of her sari around her finger. "Who will carry the chairs?"

I looked down. "What would you suggest?"

Ms. Gokhale looked at me and smiled. "How about Dumb Charades?"

"Sounds interesting!" I gasped. "We probably won't need any equipment then."

"I'll lead one of the two teams and you lead the other?"

"OK, that's the plan. I'll see you on Saturday." Feeling relieved, I hurried back to the boy's dorm.

The gathering was held in the college's botanical garden on Saturday afternoon. It was sunny with a light breeze, and cooler in the garden than it was on the grounds. Students started trickling in at about four o'clock. A group of about fifteen girls, some wearing saris and others in skirts, from the ladies dorm arrived together, giggling and chatting amongst themselves. By mid-afternoon there were about fifty students.

We played Dumb Charades first. Ms. Gokhale gathered the two teams under a tree to explain the rules of the game. "One team will select a person or an object, and after they've decided the team leader will write it on a piece of paper and pass it on to the leader of the other team. The other team's leader will provide clues to their team members using different gestures, facial expressions, and body language to help them identify the selected object within five minutes to win the round."

After answering a few questions from her audience, she assigned my team to select an object. We decided on Jawaharlal Nehru, the prime minister of India at the time. I wrote the name on a piece of paper and handed it over to Ms. Gokhale. She smiled, took the paper from me, and walked back to the other side of the garden where her team was waiting. She started describing Nehru using gestures and body language. She pretended to pull down a cap on her head. Her team started guessing. "A man, with a cap." Ms. Gokhale nodded in agreement and continued. Banging her right fist on her left palm she indicated that the man holds power. "Prime Minister Nehru!" shouted one of her team members. Ms. Gokhale gave a thumbs up sign.

Then it was my turn. Ms. Gokhale handed me a piece of paper. It read "Aawaaraa," the name of a popular Hindi movie. I was tense. I stretched my arms to indicate a wide screen; my team members shouted, "A movie!" I nodded vigorously and started acting out the pauper hero, strolling along with a stick on his shoulder. The team screamed "Raj Kapoor!" There were more than a dozen Raj Kapoor movies—I now had to make them guess *Aawaaraa* specifically; I started portraying a homeless person wandering from place to place. But time was up. Ms. Gokhale's team cheered jubilantly.

Dumb Charades was followed by a tea break. I was pleased with my own performance. In a relaxed mood I wandered around eating cake and drinking tea. My nervousness had vanished. My friends and I talked not only with Ms. Gokhale, but also with other girls who were with her. Everyone was happy and wanted Dnyana Sadhana to organize more such functions.

5

MADE IN HEAVEN?

I began my second year at the college in late June 1956. On the last Sunday of the month about a dozen boys gathered in the common room of the boys' dorm to elect Dnyana Sadhana's executive committee. Half a dozen girls from the ladies' dorm also attended the meeting. One of them in a light blue sari caught my attention. Tall and slim with a broad forehead, sharp eyebrows, fair skin, and a joyful smile, she was a knockout. The girls sat on one side of the room and the boys on the other side. It was not much of an election. I offered to be the general secretary. The girl in the blue sari, who introduced herself as Saroj Joshi, volunteered to be the joint secretary. I was pleased at the prospect of getting to interact with her. At the end of the meeting, I approached Saroj and said, "Let's meet next week to chalk out the functions for the year."

Saroj smiled and said, "Let's meet tomorrow. Around five?"

The next day, I walked over to the girls' dorm. Instead of talking at the gate, Saroj suggested that we sit down in the visitors' room of the dorm. Saroj was from Mumbai. She had moved into the ladies' dorm at the start of the academic year. After making plans for the upcoming year, I asked, "Saroj, why did you opt for Fergusson? There are many good colleges in Mumbai."

"It wasn't an easy decision," she answered, looking down at her purse on the coffee table. "But Mumbai's humidity isn't good for my health."

"How so?"

"I was a tuberculosis patient, like my father. He succumbed to the illness."

"I'm so sorry," I said.

Saroj looked out the window. "My mother was worried about me. She consulted a doctor. He advised that I move to a dry climate."

"If you fully recover will you return to Mumbai?"

"Most likely."Saroj smiled.

"I wish you well, but I'd miss you." I looked at her. "You seem to be in good health."

She blushed. Looking into my eyes she said, "Let's wait and see. You never know—Mumbai isn't far from Pune."

We met often to work out the details of the Dnyana Sadhana functions but always discussed personal matters as well—our plans for education, our families, and our school activities. These meetings often lasted for an hour or so. At the end of the academic year, Saroj returned to Mumbai, and I traveled to Dhule.

I returned to the college in June and was disappointed not to see Saroj at the first meeting of Dnyana Sadhana. Her friend told me that Saroj had registered at a college in Mumbai. The same evening, I wrote her a letter saying I'd missed her and describing two upcoming Dnyana Sadhana functions that I thought she would have enjoyed. One was a reading of famous Pune-based Marathi poets, who were going to present their popular poems. The other was the next annual gathering day; a popular Marathi novelist had been invited as the guest of honour. At the end of the letter I asked if I could visit her and meet her family sometime in July.

I was surprised when I received a letter from Saroj. Most families in those days were very conservative, generally discouraging a daughter's correspondence with a boy not known to them, but Saroj wrote: "We all discuss the events of the day at the dinner table. I showed your letter to my mother. She encouraged me to invite you for lunch. Let me know when you can possibly come over. We have nothing planned for the weekends next month. Just select any Sunday that will suit you." She gave detailed directions on how to reach her place from the nearest local train station.

The following Sunday morning, I caught a seven o'clock train to Mumbai. The train passed through dark tunnels in the mountains, slowing down to negotiate the hilly curves, winding around lush green slopes, over hovering bridges and meandering tracks. Every few minutes I saw another spectacular waterfall gushing down the walls of a valley. But my thoughts wandered around Saroj and her family. How would her mother react to me? Would Saroj be comfortable with my visit?

In Mumbai, I took a local train and reached Saroj's house around eleven-thirty. It was a three-storey building on a small, narrow lot. It looked to have been recently built, a new concrete structure compared to the old dilapidated buildings on the street surrounding it. Saroj had mentioned that they lived on the top floor. I climbed two flights of stairs and rang the doorbell. Saroj opened the door. She looked pleased but flustered. "Oh, Jagannath, you're earlier than I expected!"

"Your directions were perfect. I didn't even have to stop and ask for help."

"Come in," Saroj waved me into the hallway.

It was a small apartment; the hallway leading to the living room had windows on one side and a bathroom and kitchen on the other. The living room clearly doubled as a bedroom. Saroj's mother was in the kitchen standing beside the stove.

"Mom, meet my friend Jagannath from Fergusson," said Saroj.

"How was your journey, Jagannath?" her mother asked.

"It was comfortable. The train wasn't crowded."

"Lunch will be ready soon. I'll join you in the living room in a few minutes." She lifted the lid on a pot of curry and gave it a stir.

When I wandered into the living room, I saw two straight-back wooden chairs, a desk and a cot. Aruna, Saroj's younger sister, was sitting at the desk doing her homework. An enlarged photo of Saroj's father hung on the wall. "Hello," Aruna said, waving her hand toward the books. "I'm almost done with my homework."

"I can help you, if it's math," I said.

"No, it's social studies." Aruna put away her books and sat down beside Saroj at the edge of the cot. The two of them were almost identical except that Aruna was at least four inches shorter than her sister, and she was wearing a schoolgirl's skirt instead of a sari.

I made myself comfortable in one of the chairs. Aruna was a chatterbox. She started telling me about a Marathi movie, Shyamchi Aai (Shyam's mother), which had been awarded the gold medal by the president of India. Aruna had watched the movie with Saroj in a local movie theatre. While I was listening to Aruna, Saroj's mother called us for lunch. She had fair skin like her daughters, and she was between the two girls in height. She wore a white nine-yard sari, the traditional dress for a widow.

"Lunch is very simple; I hope you like it," she said as she dished up the food.

"Oh! Potato curry! That's my favourite," I said delightedly.

"Saroj should have asked you what you like."

"I'm not fussy, as long as it's vegetarian."

The food was delicious. Aruna was busy eating and there was no more talk about the movie. Saroj said to her mother, "Jagannath is shy; serve him more potato curry."

As we ate, I asked Saroj's mother, "How should I address you? Would Mawashi be OK?" (Mawashi means aunt.)

"That's fine. All of Saroj's and Aruna's friends call me Mawashi."

Saroj turned to me, suddenly excited. "I've taken up a part-time job in a bank. I attend the college in the morning and work at the bank in the afternoon," she said.

"Saroj pays for her own education. It's such a relief to me," Mawashi said proudly.

"I wish I could follow her example," I said, feeling jealous of Saroj. "But science subjects, my physics and statistics courses, require lab attendance besides lectures. I can't take afternoons off like you."

"I do have the advantage of being in sociology," Saroj said.

"I think my father would try to prevent me from taking a part-time job, anyway."

"Why?" asked Mawashi.

"He wants me to concentrate on my studies and not worry about money."

Mawashi nodded. "He must be a rich man."

"Not really, but our family earns enough from farming."

"How many in your family?" Mawashi was inquisitive.

"I have six brothers and one sister. I'm the eldest."

"Oh, yours is a big family." Mawashi couldn't hide her surprise. It was already four o'clock. Mawashi got up and announced, "It is tea time; continue your conversation. I shall join you once the tea is ready."

I said, "I'll leave after tea. I don't want to miss my train."

After enjoying tea and snacks I got up and started putting on my sandals. Everyone followed me to the door.

"It was so nice to see you, Jagannath," said Saroj. "It's been too long."

"It was a pleasure to have you with us. Come back soon," said Mawashi.

"I would like to," I said, starting to wave too early.

My thoughts stayed with Saroj and her family all the way back to Pune. I was happy that Mawashi had been so warm. I thought I could probably go to visit Saroj again as soon as I wanted.

We kept in touch through letters and occasional visits. Finally, over a year after we'd met, I decided to make a surprise visit and propose to her. It was an impulsive decision. On a Sunday, in February 1958, during my final year of a BSc, I took the train to Mumbai, as I'd done many times before, and arrived at Saroj's apartment unannounced. I rang the doorbell. Aruna opened the door.

"Mom, Jagannath is here!" she announced.

"We weren't expecting you, Jagannath," said Mawashi.

For the first time, I felt nervous. "I wanted to surprise you."

"Saroj is out of town." Mawashi seemed distracted.

"Oh really?"

"She wanted to attend a little get-together with friends from her Fergusson dorm."

"Is she getting back today?"

"She planned to return tomorrow morning. I hope she does."

I tried to keep smiling, "Oh? Why?"

"An Indian army officer is visiting with the possibility of a marriage proposal," Mawashi said gleefully.

I could not respond immediately. I felt sick. Finally, I said, "Doesn't she know about it?"

"No, we received a phone call after Saroj left."

"I wish I had known about her plans," I said.

"Never mind, I'm glad to see you. Would you like to join us for lunch? It's ready."

I swallowed hard. "Thanks, it would be my pleasure."

Aruna set the table and Mawashi served up rice with lentil curry on top, chapatti, mixed vegetables, and fresh vegetable salad. I gulped rather than relishing the food. After lunch, Aruna told me about her Kathak dance class and tried to demonstrate her dancing skills. I couldn't concentrate. As soon as she was finished I had to leave to catch my afternoon train to Pune.

I tried to console myself. Saroj was twenty-two. If I was honest with myself, her family was being practical in looking for a well-settled life partner, a steady income earner for her. I was still a student, just about to finish my undergraduate degree before going for a master's degree in statistics—I would be studying for another two years. Who knows what the situation would be when I finished my education and got a decent job? There is many a slip between the cup and the lip!

A few days later, I received a letter from Saroj that pulled me out of my gloom. She wrote:

Mom told me about your surprise visit. You came all the way from Pune and we didn't see each other! Why didn't you drop me a line? I would have told you about my plans. Next month we'll both be busy preparing for final exams, but please spare some time to write me.

P.S. The proposal from the army officer didn't work out; his family didn't like that he was two years younger than me.

The postscript sparked hope in me, but I decided to be practical rather than emotional. At the end of June I travelled to Pune to join the University of Pune for a master's degree in statistics, as planned. I kept exchanging letters with Saroj but visited her only once during the second half of 1958.

One Saturday in December 1958 after my classes, I returned to my apartment and found a letter on the floor. Hoping it was from Saroj, I picked it up. It turned out to be from my father, who wrote that Ram Alai and his two uncles from Nampur had visited my parents and offered me a marriage proposal for Ram's sister Krishna. Nana concluded, "We have to reciprocate the visit. Let me know which dates are convenient to you for the visit. Of all the proposals so far, I would say that this is the best."

The letter was a bolt out of the blue. I did not know how to respond. I had heard about Krishna's late father, nicknamed "Baglanche Baba," who had passed away seven years before. He was a freedom fighter in the struggle for India's independence, and a visionary too. He set up industries, including a cotton ginning plant and a sugar cane processing plant to produce jaggery (a solidified molasses), in his small town of Nampur, creating employment opportunities for the local youth. He also owned vast tracts of farmland. The total annual farm levy he paid to the government was the highest in the three surrounding districts.

Krishna's family background could not have been better. I was confused. At the end of two years I would be ready to propose to Saroj. But by then her family might have found her a more suitable match. I had not expressed my love for Saroj. Did she have similar feelings about me—or was she apprehensive about my rural background and uneducated family living in a small town? Perhaps she liked me only as a friend, and I would have to finally opt for an arranged marriage anyway. In two years there might be no better prospect than Krishna. My confusion grew more and more and my head started hurting. I went for a long walk. The fresh air did seem to help, and after a while I decided to think with my head and not with my heart. Instead of procrastinating, I replied to my father and told him I could take advantage of the Republic Day holiday, Monday, January 26, and make the trip to Dhule.

My father informed Krishna's family that we would visit them on Sunday. A team of four—my father, my high school teacher Aabaa Deshpande, my cousin Vishnu (a primary school teacher), and I—travelled by bus to Nampur. Ram and his uncle Govind, Baba's stepbrother, were waiting to receive us. Ram looked to be about my age. He was dressed all in white: plain shirt, pajama, and a slightly tilted Gandhi cap on his head. Govind was in a traditional white dhoti, a white shirt and a white cap. He was a follower of Gandhi's philosophy of cottage industry, and his clothes were all hand-spun and hand-woven. Because he was hard of hearing, he carried a slate for communication. Ram came forward and offered to carry our bags.

Govind clearly wanted to impress us. After breakfast he took us on a tour of the family residence complex. The complex was a huge edifice shared by a joint family of six cousins—Baba, as the head, his step-brother Govind, and four cousins. We were shown two massive main entrance gates wide enough to allow bullock carts loaded with farm goods to enter into the open yard of the complex. Besides the two main gates, there were separate side entrances to the living quarters of the each of the six cousins. In the centre of the complex there was big open space with access from each of the six wings.

Govind launched into a story about Baba's role in India's freedom struggle. "Many freedom fighters went into hiding to avoid arrest by the British rulers." He looked over to make sure his words were having the intended effect. "They had to keep moving from place to place. Baba helped them. He sheltered many of them in our residence complex." We were approaching another gate. "In the event of a police raid, the intricacy of the complex was a great help. It made it easy for the freedom fighters to escape using one of half a dozen exits."

The purpose of our visit was to meet Krishna, check her educational background, and get an idea of her personality. It was kind of an interview. Later we followed Govind into one of the spacious halls in the Baba's wing of the complex. The walls were decorated with a portrait of Baba and a few of his photographs with some well-known Congress Party leaders like Sardar Patel and Lokmanya Tilak. All of us, including Krishna's three uncles and her brother, sat on the carpet in a semicircle with our backs to the windows. Krishna was supposed to sit in front of us facing the window so that the groom's party should have a clear view of the prospective bride.

Govind left for a moment to invite Krishna into the hall. Wearing a lime green sari and a smile on her face, Krishna stepped in from the adjoining room. She was slim and good looking with fair skin—not short, but not as tall as Saroj. What impressed me the most was the way she walked into the hall with confidence visible on her radiant face. Govind asked her to take a seat in front of us.

Complexion plays a crucial role in arranged marriages, particularly for girls. In the 1950s, there was a craze for fair-skinned brides in India. Cosmetic companies produced lightening creams and perfumed bleach packs promising the user the complexion of a famous movie actress. An artificial fair complexion was not only expensive, but also posed a serious health risk due to harmful cosmetics ingredients.

My father and Aabaa started the interview with a few routine questions about Krishna's education and relatives. Vishnu then took the lead, proving his skills as a primary school teacher. I was just listening and looking at Krishna. Vishnu handed her a newspaper and asked her to read aloud the headline news about the opening of a cooperative sugar factory by the chief minister of the state. After she did so, Vishnu posed her questions related to the article: Who inaugurated the factory? What is his designation? Who were on the dais with him? Krishna, looking gleefully at Vishnu, answered everything correctly.

"Do you attend ladies' get-togethers during religious festivals?" Vishnu asked.

"Yes, I do," She said assertively.

"Suppose you want to organize one. Could you please draft an invitation?"

"Sure, let me try."

Someone handed Krishna a piece of paper and a pencil, and in about ten minutes, she composed a neatly drafted invitation letter.

Handing it back, she said, "Do you have any more questions?"

Krishna's question was a surprise to all of us. We all looked at each other to know if anyone wanted to ask a question. Since no one came forward, Aabaa said, "No, you may go now."

Krishna respectfully bowed to everyone and walked back into the adjoining room.

After lunch we headed to the bus terminal to catch the four o'clock bus. Ram and his uncles came with us to say good-bye. Govind wrote on his slate, "Let us know your decision soon." He showed it to my father and looked at him. My father nodded his head and gestured to indicate that he understood. On the way back, Nana asked me for my decision. I gave my consent.

In the evening I caught the train back to Pune. The train passed from one station to another as my mind wandered from one past event to the next. I recalled the advice one of my teachers gave my father: "For a cart to run smoothly, the two wheels have to be the same size; the same applies in marriages too. The two partners have to be compatible." In terms of academic education, we were incompatible; I was studying for a postgraduate degree and Krishna didn't go beyond elementary school.

The two families consulted a priest. He opened the page for the month of May in his lunar calendar, made some calculations regarding the positions of the planets, and declared, "The evening of Sunday, May 31, 1959 would be an auspicious time for the wedding."

The wedding took place in Nampur. On the evening on May 30, our family, relatives and friends descended on Nampur. We were accommodated in a huge family temple with an inner sanctuary where the primary deity was housed with a big congregation hall in front of it. The congregation hall became a dormitory with mattresses spread around for the guests to sleep at night.

The wedding ceremony the next day was conducted in the living room of Krishna's family home with the invited guests seated in a pandal (a temporary structure covered with fabric) Krishna's family had specially erected in front of the house. Krishna and I sat facing each other surrounded by a few youngsters and the priest. At five-thirty in the afternoon the priest started reciting a mangalashtak (sacred eight stanzas) invoking all the planets, gods, and goddesses to bless us with a happy and healthy married life. His monotone recitation was played through loudspeakers in the pandal. At the end of each stanza, the priest was making us aware of our new responsibilities as a wedded couple. As soon as the priest concluded the last stanza he signalled to the orchestra.

There was a loud outburst of music announcing that the wedding had taken place and it was time for the groom and bride to exchange garlands. I put a garland of red roses around Krishna's neck. Then it was Krishna's turn. She did not reach out to put the garland around my neck—she simply threw it at me. The garland fell down at my feet.

I was shocked. I wondered if I should walk out of the ceremony. The chaos it would cause amongst the hundreds of guests if I did was nothing compared to the predicament it would put both families in. None of my family members had witnessed the incident; they were all outside in the pandal.

I calmly picked up the garland and put it around my neck.

6

NEW HOME, NEW NAMES

Of a half a dozen post-wedding ceremonies stretching into the wee hours, the last one was vidai (adieu), sending the bride off to her new family. We loaded the bus with our luggage; everyone took their seats. Kamalini, my parents and I were standing at the entrance to the bus. Eyes filled with tears, Krishna's family gathered around us to say goodbye to her, throwing in last-minute advice on how to conduct herself in her new home. Krishna's mother turned to my mother and pleaded, "Krishna is young; please guide her if she makes any mistakes." My mother assured her, "I will treat Krishna like my daughter. We'll make her happy." During the process of vidai brides usually sob and hug their family members, but Krishna's face remained expressionless during the entire ceremony. I wondered, *why?*

We arrived back in Dhule around noon on June 1. My mother placed a pot full of rice at the front entrance of the house. Krishna tipped it over with her feet, spilling the rice on the floor as she entered her new home. This ritual signifies to the new bride that no one will mind any inadvertent mistakes in her daily routine; she need not be on her guard all the time.

The following day, we held the religious ceremony called Lakshmi Pooja, the worship of Lakshmi, the goddess of abundance, in the living room hall. Traditionally, the ceremony is an occasion to rename the bride and announce that she is now looked upon as the Goddess Lakshmi, the source of abundance and happiness in the house. She is taken around the house by her mother-in-law and shown everything in each room and assured that she will have access to it all.

Before we started the ceremony, I said to Krishna, "You will have a new last name now, but I'm not fussy about changing your first name. We don't have to follow the tradition."

"Do you have any particular name in mind?" Krishna asked with curiosity.

"Kamalini."

"I like it." Krishna smiled.

"Are you sure?"

"I never liked the name Krishna, but I had no choice."

I wanted Krishna to have the freedom of choosing her new name. I asked her, "Would you prefer any name other than Kamalini?"

"No, I'm Kamalini from now on."

While Krishna was being given the tour of the house, I sat in the adjoining room all by myself with a silver platter on the table in front of me and three bowls filled with different coloured rice grains. Using the coloured grains I wrote "Kamalini" on the silver platter and covered it with a fancy scarf. When Krishna returned, I brought the silver platter to the living room hall where the rest of the family and the guests were waiting. I removed the scarf and the priest read the name aloud. As everyone applauded, I announced, "Krishna left her parents' home and is now entering her new home as Kamalini."

The next day, Kamalini and I registered our marriage. The middle aged registrar, who could not have seemed less interested in his job, entered the marriage in his records without bothering to examine whether we had attained the legal age for marriage. Years later, I discovered that the Hindu Marriage Act 1955 sets the minimum age for marriage for women at eighteen and for men at twenty-one. Kamalini was not even seventeen on the day of the wedding—she would have turned seventeen in another twenty-three days. Had I been familiar with the legislation at the time, I would have insisted on putting the wedding on hold for a year. However, under the Act such marriages were voidable but not void; they become valid after the bride turned 18, unless she sought a declaration of the marriage as void.

A few days after the wedding, Kamalini and I had finished our lunch and were chatting in our bedroom. I asked Kamalini, "Have you ever read about Jyotiba and Savitri Phule?"

"No. What about them?" Kamalini asked looking at me.

"Jyotiba was a social reformer interested in women's education. His wife Savitri was uneducated, but after their marriage, Jyotiba taught her to read and write. In 1848 she became the first female teacher at the first women's school in India."

"Why are you telling me this?"

"I'd like you to resume your education."

"I have no desire to go back to school," Kamalini seemed disturbed.

"It would give you opportunities."

"But your parents won't like the idea."

"I'll convince them." I tried to reassure her.

"I cook for a family of eleven, plus two farm labourers. When would I find time to study?" Kamalini challenged me.

"I'll arrange to have you relieved of the cooking."

She started fiddling with her bracelets. "It's been more than four years since I attended school."

"If my sister is getting an education beyond grade seven, why not my wife?"

"There's a difference between a daughter and a daughter-in-law." Kamalini retorted.

"There doesn't have to be! Pushpa will be in grade eight, and you can join her in the same class. You can be company for each other and study together."

"It will be embarrassing for me to study with girls four years younger. Let us not discuss this anymore."

Kamalini came up with all kinds of excuses. I was not only frustrated with Kamalini's excuses, but I was also disappointed to realize that she had no academic ambition.

A week later, I received a letter from Saroj. She congratulated me and asked about the wedding, whether I could send her a photograph. I shared the letter with Kamalini. "Who is this Saroj?" Kamalini asked. I candidly told her about how I had met Saroj, and how I had intended to marry her. I was not surprised when Kamalini asked, "Do you regret it?"

"No. Once I make a decision, I don't look back." I folded the letter and put it back on the desk.

"Is she married?"

"No."

"How often do you meet her?" Kamalini wanted to dig further into the matter.

"I haven't since we got engaged."

"Do you still communicate with her?"

"I do, just like I would with any of my friends."

"What's there to communicate?" Kamalini asked tersely, looking into my eyes.

"Things just like what you read in her letter."

"Saroj seems to be a straightforward person." Kamalini seemed satisfied.

Looking intently into her eyes, I said, "I answered your questions. Now let me ask you a question."

"What?"

"Why did you throw the garland at me during the wedding ceremony?"

"I could not reach you to put the garland around your neck." Kamalini was avoiding my eyes.

"You didn't think it was insulting?" I could feel myself losing my patience.

"No, I had no choice."

"Didn't you think it might affect our relationship?"

"I wasn't thinking. I did it at the spur of the moment." Kamalini seemed confused, almost blindsided by my unexpected questions.

"I could have called off the wedding right at that moment, but I controlled myself so as not to upset everyone."

Kamalini did not respond; instead she just looked in the other direction. Though this was a painful dialogue, I maintained my cool. I could have walked out of the room; but I did not want Kamalini to feel guilty.

The conversation pulled me back in the past. My first marriage proposal came along when I was hardly ten. It was nine o'clock on a bright sunny day, and I was getting ready for school. I was in grade three. I needed help finding my books, but my mother was busy in the kitchen and Aai, my grandmother, was engrossed in her prayers. My father was talking to some visitors in the living room. I started screaming and banging on the kitchen door. He excused himself and came to me.

"Could you please calm down, Jagan?" my father asked me.

I stopped yelling and stared at his authoritative look.

"We have some guests. They want to talk to you."

"Why?"

"They have brought a marriage proposal for you."

I looked up to Nana and asked, "What does that mean?"

"Don't ask questions. Just come to the living room."

I walked into the living room and sat down on the carpet in front of two strangers wearing dark jackets and black caps. My father sat down beside them.

The lower halves of our living room walls were painted dark red and the upper halves white. The teak pillars in the wall were darkened with oil every year to protect them against termites. The carpet along all three walls in the room was lined with long, round white cushions with big square ones on top. The visitors were sitting against the cushions, and their black caps blended perfectly with the black teak pillars.

"What's your name?" one of them asked.

I thought it was a silly question, but I quietly answered, "Jagannath."

"What grade are you in?" asked the other guest, looking at me.

"Grade three."

"What's your teacher's name?"

"Mr. Mudawadkar."

"You may go now. Get ready for school." The first guest gestured giving me permission to go.

I got up to leave, but stopped and hung around the doorway. I called Aai to find my school bag, glancing back into the living room.

"I would like my daughter to marry your son," said the girl's father.

"My son and your daughter are both too young to get married," my father responded firmly.

"Let's go just for an engagement; the marriage could take place later," said the guest.

"A long gap between the engagement and the marriage is not desirable," said my father.

The guests turned to Aai, who had come in after me with my school bag in hand.

"It would be nice if an engagement took place in your lifetime."

"I leave it to Bandu to decide," responded Aai, pointing to Nana.

The kind of arrangement the guests suggested was not uncommon in our community during those days, but my father was firm in his decision. I was amused by the whole episode; I neither knew the meaning of "engagement" nor of the word "marriage".

I was in grade nine. One day, at about five o'clock I had just returned home from the school and was heading to the kitchen for chevada (spicy puffed rice) and a laddu (a ball-shaped Indian sweet) before heading out to the gym. I had barely entered the kitchen when I heard my father's voice behind me.

"We have two visitors wanting to meet you."

"What for? I'll be late for my workout." I said, trying not to sound annoyed.

"Nothing will happen if you're late on one day."

"OK, but who are the visitors?"

"They have a marriage proposal for you. The girl's father and his lawyer brother are waiting in the living room." Nana whispered softly.

"Why can't you tell them that I'm not ready for a marriage proposal? I'm only in grade nine."

"Let's not discuss this now. Be polite and meet them. Finish your snacks and come into the living room." Nana said in a tone that left no room for discussion.

As I walked into the living room, I looked at the portrait of Aai on the wall. My father had commissioned it after she died and it always reminded me of her love for me. I sat down cross-legged, facing the two gentlemen wearing traditional dress, white dhotis, dark jackets, and black caps. My father sat down beside them.

"Jagannath, did we catch you at a bad time?" asked one of them. He must be the lawyer I guessed.

"That's OK. I was just on my way to the gym."

"What do you do there?"

"We do gymnastics on the single bar and double bar, and malkhamb. I go with three of my friends." (Malkhamb is a traditional Indian sport in which a gymnast performs feats and poses around a vertical wooden pole.)

"Do you also participate in any games?" The other man was quietly listening; letting his elder brother carry on the conversation.

"I'm on the kho-kho team at school. We compete in inter-school tournaments." I said with pride. (Kho-kho is South Asia's popular tag sport.)

"We won't hold you up for too long. I hear that you're at the top of your class. What subjects do you like?"

"I like algebra and geometry the most."

"What would you like to be in life?" The lawyer probed further.

"I haven't thought about it. But I like teaching."

"Why teaching?" asked the girl's father, participating for the first time in the conversation.

"I'm the class monitor. Whenever a teacher is late or on leave, I get to lead the class and solve math problems for my classmates."

"Have you ever thought about becoming a doctor?" asked the lawyer.

"Not really."

"Why?"

Everyone in the room was looking at me with curiosity to listen to my answer. I said, "Medical education begins with dissecting frogs. I hate killing animals."

"You may change your opinion later," said the lawyer.

"Maybe, but I don't think so." I responded, thinking that the lawyer was too inquisitive.

"Do you take part in any other extracurricular activities?"

"I like to enter essay competitions."

"Have you won any?"

"Yes, I was the winner of two annual essay competitions sponsored by the school."

"What were the topics?"

"'Will a war lead to world peace?' and 'Desirability of the linguistic division of India.'"

"Do you also participate in debating competitions?"

"No, I have stage fright. May I be excused? My friends are waiting for me."

"Best of luck, Jagannath! You may go." The lawyer seemed satisfied with my performance and gave me his whole hearted best wishes.

Later that night, my father told me about the conversation that took place after I left.

"Jagannath is a bright student," the lawyer had said to my father. "Though he doesn't like the study of medicine, he will make a good doctor."

"He would need lots of money for a medical education. I wouldn't be able to afford it," my father said.

"If you take my niece to be his bride, you need not worry about the money. We'll take care of it."

"A girl from an educated family such as yours will find it hard to adjust to our farming family," my father said.

"I don't believe so."

"You may be right, but I would wait until Jagannath at least finishes high school."

———————

A year later, a businessman from a nearby town approached us with a marriage proposal for his daughter. Unlike the lawyer, he did not come with a career plan for me. Instead, he casually asked, "Let me see your right-hand palm, Jagannath." I held my palm out in front of him. For a minute or two, he looked at it intensely. "Bandu, this boy is going to make a career in education and will excel in it," he said to my father, who was sitting beside him.

I was amused by the guest's predictions and glad that he saw a career in education for me. My father was fascinated; he said, "Palmistry looks to be your hobby."

"Yes, I know a little bit about it, but I'm not an expert." The business-man looked at my father and responded in a humble tone.

"What else do you see in his future?"

"He will enjoy good health and a long life."

"What about getting a beautiful wife?" I asked jokingly.

"It's a secret. I won't divulge it," the man laughed.

When he formally asked my father about a marriage proposal, once again my father politely said, "I would prefer to wait until Jagannath completes his high school diploma."

A neighbour nicknamed "Appa" lived a few doors down the road from us. He was in his late forties and worked as a clerk in a government office. Every Sunday he would drop in to see my parents and chat about the happenings in the neighbourhood. One Sunday after dinner, he dropped in as usual, but instead of launching into neighbourhood talk, he said to my father, "Bandu, I would like you to consider my niece as a bride for Jagannath."

My father responded the same way he always did. "It's too early to think about it."

"It's a standing proposal. Let me know whenever you are ready."

"I will." My father proudly said.

"My niece Kausalya is a pretty girl. She's also a good cook and a good help to her mother with the housekeeping. She will be a great asset to your family."

I was amused by the name Kausalya, which is the name of the mother of Lord Rama, the hero of *Ramayana*, but I wondered whether Appa was promoting Kausalya as a helping hand to my mother or a bride for me.

———————

Child marriages were illegal but common in many communities in

India. My father did not accept any of the marriage proposals that started arriving when I was ten. After I finished my high school diploma there was a break of almost five years in the chain of marriage proposals. Kamalini's proposal was a bombshell. My father looked at it very favourably and I consented.

A few days after the euphoria of all the ceremonies had subsided, one evening my cousin Vishnu dropped in to have chat with me. I had finished my supper and was browsing through the evening newspaper in the living room.

"After you accepted her proposal, Kamalini's uncle Govind, her brother Ram and Nathu came to Dhule to negotiate the dowry and jewelry for the bride." Vishnu said, pulling me months back into the past.

"Who is Nathu?" I asked, a little contemptuously.

"The father-in-law of Ram."

"He wasn't involved in anything earlier."

Vishnu shrugged. "I guess Ram brought him along as a senior person for advice."

"The dowry shouldn't have been an issue at all."

"It is a tradition. I opened by suggesting six thousand rupees. Govind wrote five thousand on his slate and showed it to Ram. Then Nathu grabbed the slate, erased it, and suggested we break and resume negotiations the following day."

"Didn't you smell a rat when Nathu suggested postponing the negotiations?"

Vishnu was piqued by my question. "We were caught off guard. Nathu took off alone and went to a neighbour's house for the night."

"What happened to the rest of the group?" I asked.

"The next morning the neighbour invited Ram and his uncle for breakfast. We were waiting for Ram and the rest of them to return to continue the discussion, but they didn't show up."

"All of you should've realized that Nathu wasn't acting in good faith."

"I know. Uncle was concerned that the failed negotiations would send a wrong signal to the community, lead to gossip. He wanted me to ask the neighbour what had happened."

"I would have liked Ram to go fly a kite," I blustered. "He didn't even have the guts to stand up against his father-in-law."

"I had to respect Uncle's feelings." Vishnu looked at me. "When I went to the neighbour, he told me that Ram and his group went to a nearby town to look for another match for Krishna."

"Don't you think you should have consulted me in the matter?"

"Uncle didn't want you to get upset. Nathu suggested the neighbour's son, Murali, as a match for Krishna. But Ram didn't want his fair-skinned sister to get married to a black boy like Murali."

"Funny, in the dorms, Murali was usually mistaken for an international student from Africa."

"When he saw Ram's reaction, the neighbour directed them to another boy."

"What happened next?" I expressed my curiosity.

"Someone phoned Narayan, Krishna's brother-in-law, and told him what was happening. Narayan was furious. It turned out that Ram had given the cold shoulder to the alternate proposal, just like he did to that of Murali. Narayan brought back Ram and his uncle by the end of the day, without Nathu. The new group under Narayan's leadership successfully completed the negotiations."

"Vishnu, all of you cheated me regarding the most important decision affecting my life; you treated me like a marketable commodity."

7

IN CANADA

In May 1960, I completed my MSc in statistics. Since I was neither distracted by wedding preparations nor upset by a dowry conflict, my performance was far better than it had been during the previous year.

I wanted to become financially independent as soon as possible, and I began to look for a job. I also wanted to do social work in adult literacy and community development in the rural areas surrounding Dhule, help my family, and provide guidance to my sister and six younger brothers. In order to accomplish all this, I was keen to find a job in my hometown.

The only job opportunity for me in Dhule was a teaching position at the local college, established by the dominant Maratha community. The members of the governing board, who controlled the selection process for all the appointments in the college, were all Maratha. I mentioned my intention to apply for a position at the college to a friend who was teaching there.

Don't waste your time," he said to me.

"Why?" I asked.

"The chairman's nephew passed the M.Sc. exams with the bare minimum score and the chairman wanted him to be the principal."

"Was the position vacant?"

"No. He just dismissed the serving principal, who was far more qualified."

My friend explained the selection process. A candidate related to a board member would get the priority irrespective of merit; he just needed to have the minimum qualifications. If no such relative was in the list of the candidates, the next choice would be a candidate from their community. An outsider would be appointed only if no one from their community was available. Not being from the Maratha community, my friend advised, I stood no chance of getting the job.

That same year the state government opened an agricultural college in Dhule. The college was looking for an instructor to teach mathematics— and as it was a government institution, appointments were based on merit. By coincidence, the principal happened to hear about my availability and offered me a limited term part-time position, beginning in July 1960.

To supplement my income, I tutored mathematics students from high schools and the local college. My day started at eight o'clock in the morning, tutoring two batches of high school students. Then I would ride my bike to the agricultural college to teach, come home for lunch, prepare lectures for two hours, and conduct tutoring sessions from four to eight o'clock in the evening. Though I got used to the hectic schedule, it was not at all enjoyable. I had very little time to spend with Kamalini, let alone on the social work I had hoped to begin in the rural areas.

My appointment at the agricultural college was to end on April 30, 1961. There was no possibility of a decent full-time job in Dhule, so I had decided to look elsewhere when I received a letter from my former professor, Dr. A.R. Kamat. He offered me a position as research assistant at the renowned Gokhale Institute of Politics and Economics in Pune, one hundred fifty kilometres from Mumbai. I gladly accepted the offer. Kamalini was delighted with the idea of living independently, away from the joint family of ten. In May 1961, I moved to Pune to begin work and Kamalini, who was pregnant, went to live with her mother in Nampur. It was customary in those days in India for a young married woman to be with her parents for her first delivery and thereafter until the baby is three months old.

On October 25, I received a letter from Kamalini. She wrote, "Our son was born on October 18. He weighed eight pounds and four ounces. He is a cute fellow. We're having a naming ceremony soon. What name would you like for him? I am looking forward to seeing you."

I wrote back, "I wish I was there with you to enjoy the birth of our son. I am eagerly waiting for the Diwali vacation, which starts on November 4 —less than a week away. I am eager to see both of you. As for the name, I suggest 'Rahul'—it means 'conqueror of all miseries.' Lord Buddha's son was also called Rahul."

As soon as the office closed on November 3, I left for Nampur and arrived there early the next morning. Kamalini was waiting for me. While her mother served me breakfast, Kamalini put Rahul in my lap saying, "Rahul, look who is here to see you!" I snapped my fingers to catch Rahul's attention and he looked at me and smiled. He had fair skin, black hair, a radiant face—my son was a handsome baby, a bundle of joy. The week passed by quickly. Kamalini and I spent as much time together as possible, though of course there were always visitors stopping in to fuss over Rahul. It was incredible how much he grew and changed over such a short time, and incredible to see Kamalini, who was still so young, taking on a motherly role. Suddenly it was time to return to Pune. It was hard to leave Kamalini and Rahul.

On December 14, I received a letter from GP. He wrote:

I have joined the well-known McGill University in Montreal. It is dubbed the Harvard of Canada. If you would like to do PhD in mathematical statistics at McGill, I will do everything possible to ensure your admission and financial assistance. In case you decide to apply, send me an official request letter as soon as possible. The decision is yours.

I had been communicating with GP regularly since I met him in June 1954. He had been guiding me through every step of my career, but this letter offered me an opportunity I'd never dreamed of. A PhD degree from a prestigious Canadian university was sure to open better career opportunities than I had been exploring in India.

I immediately sent a letter to Kamalini informing her about GP's offer. She immediately wrote back, "I am happy that you are getting an opportunity to study abroad. Eventually, this will be an opportunity for me and Rahul to visit Canada. In the meantime we shall miss seeing you."

As suggested by GP, I sent him a formal letter of application and things started to move rapidly. I received a letter of admission followed by an appointment letter as research assistant. GP also helped me in getting a travel grant of three hundred dollars. He advised me to travel by ship from Mumbai to London instead of flying from Mumbai to Montreal via London. "This," he wrote, "will provide you with an opportunity to improve your English." Following GP's advice, I booked my passage to London on the SS *Stratheden*, sailing from Mumbai on August 10.

When Rahul was three months old, my parents invited Kamalini and Rahul to stay with them so they could enjoy their first grandchild. I traveled to Dhule to see Kamalini and Rahul over a weekend at the end of March. I brought a plush brown teddy bear for Rahul, and when I showed it to him he grabbed it from my hand. He was a happy, healthy, five-month old baby. He held tight to the teddy bear and tried to put it in his mouth. My father, Nana, was sitting beside me. He said, "We have planned Rahul's first haircut ceremony for April 18. Would you come?" Nana looked at me eagerly.

"I won't get leave so soon again; just go ahead without me." Rahul was in my lap; I looked at him and said, "Is it OK, Rahul?" He smiled.

Assuming everything would happen as planned, I returned to Pune. On April 23, I received a letter from Nana. I opened it, looking forward to reading about Rahul's haircut ceremony. The letter read, "I don't know how to tell you, but all of a sudden Rahul passed away on April 17. Kamalini is crying day and night. Please come to be with her as soon as possible."

Nana did not mention the cause of Rahul's death. With tears in my eyes, I went to see my supervisor Dr. Kamat and told him what had happened. He told me to go to Dhule immediately to be with Kamalini. I caught the night train. The other passengers slept; some even snored, but Rahul's face haunted me all night and I cried and could not sleep. How could this happen so suddenly? Rahul had been perfectly healthy when I saw him two weeks ago. I vividly recalled how happy he was when he grabbed the brown teddy bear I had brought for him.

I arrived in Dhule in the morning. Kamalini broke down on seeing me. She could not say a word. Nana spoke for her.

"Rahul was fine until the sixteenth. We had made all the arrangements for his ceremonial haircut. On the morning of the seventeenth, he had high fever. We called the doctor and he diagnosed it as meningitis. He couldn't help."

"I couldn't do anything for Rahul," I said, unable to stop sobbing. "Don't blame yourself. Destiny was not kind to us," Nana said sympathetically. Kamalini was quiet with tears in her eyes.

I wanted Kamalini to be out of the house where Rahul had died. I asked her to get ready to join me in Pune and we caught the bus the next day. In Pune, we rented a one-bedroom apartment about a ten minute bike ride from my office. I had many friends in Pune from my college days. On weekends we would exchange visits with them over lunch or supper. Once in a while we enjoyed going to movies. Immersed in the new circle of friends, Kamalini got over her grief.

June 30 was my last day at the Gokhale Institute. On July 1 Kamalini and I left for a week-long vacation which included a sightseeing tour of the famous caves of Ajanta and Ellora, and Bibi-ka-Muqbara, known as the "Taj of Deccan." Prince Azam Shah, son of Mogul Emperor Aurangzeb, built this mausoleum in memory of his mother.

The tourist season was just about over and we could enjoy the caves without pushing through crowds of tourists. We were joined by another couple and together we hired a tourist guide to show us the caves. The vacation was, in a way, our belated honeymoon. The concept of a honeymoon was alien in our families—this was the first quality time we had enjoyed together. Kamalini was overjoyed. Having grown up in an orthodox, conservative family, she never had been on a sightseeing tour. While going through the Ajanta caves, she said, "This is the first time ever in my life to go sightseeing. Our school never organized any field trips." She grinned up at me. "I am really thrilled to see these beautiful caves."

During our vacation I casually mentioned to Kamalini that I was short on funds for my trip to Canada.

"How much?" she asked.

"At least fifteen hundred rupees."

"Let's sell my jewelry and get the cash for it."

Kamalini surprised me with her offer. "But it's your jewelry," I said. "It's your wedding gift. I have no right to it."

"Aren't we supposed to solve our problems together?"

"Thanks a lot, Kamal," I said tightly embracing her.

Reluctantly, I sold the jewelry for fifteen hundred rupees. (Five years later I bought sixteen ounces of gold for Kamalini and she used it to design new jewelry, which she then had made by a goldsmith.)

After the vacation, we started a round of visits to various relatives. I was the first person within our community to travel abroad. Everyone felt proud of me, offering their congratulations at public meetings in their towns. The teachers in my old high school were also excited; the headmaster officially invited me to address the students and share my thoughts with them. Seven hundred students were seated in twenty rows of thirty-five each in an open playground. When the headmaster recounted my unique performance at the SSC examination, the students received it with a big round of applause. I told the students how I was looking forward to studying at the prestigious McGill University in Canada and about the necessary preparations for moving to North America. I concluded by wishing them success in their studies. Addressing such a big crowd was something new for me, but I found it to be an enjoyable experience.

After almost three hectic weeks of public meetings we arrived in Mumbai on August 7. We spent the day with Saroj, shopping for things I needed to bring to Canada, and afterwards, she invited us for dinner at her place. Her mother was delighted to see us. She had prepared my favourite potato curry. For dessert she served us fruit salad. Kamalini and I both enjoyed Mawashi's good cooking. Before we left for the hotel, Saroj stopped me. "I'm happy that you are going to Canada to study. But don't forget us," she joked.

"How can I? I shall definitely write you once I get settled."

"What about me?" Kamalini, putting on her shoes in front of me, teased.

"Of course, you will be the first on my list, followed by Saroj," I smiled, looking at her.

"What time do you sail?" Saroj asked.

"Twelve noon; but I'll have to board the boat at least an hour before."

"I'll come to see you off."

Visitors kept coming to the hotel to wish me a good voyage. By eleven o'clock at night, we were exhausted and retired to our room. Kamalini, who was pregnant with our second child, was sad. "Once again you will not be with me when our baby will be born." Kamalini said with tears in her eyes.

"I know; I shall try my best to get you and our baby to Canada as soon as possible," I said. Just then someone knocked on the door. It was midnight.

"I have travelled three hundred kilometres to wish you a happy journey," the well-wisher announced. Though I was angry internally, I kept my cool and thanked him and closed the door.

By eight-thirty in the morning on August 10, I was all packed and ready to go to the boat terminal. The feeling of separation hit me hard as we left the hotel room. That was the last moment we had any privacy—after leaving the room we were going to be surrounded with relatives and friends waiting to join us on our way to the boat terminus. When we arrived at the Ballard Pier, it was crowded with the friends and families of many others like me getting ready to board the ship. About seventy relatives and friends had arrived to give me a send-off. Our group found a corner where we all could come together. Kamalini's brother had organized a photo session, but since all seventy people could not be included in a single photo, the photographer divided us in two groups—one consisting of my parents, brothers and close relatives, and the other consisting of my friends.

There was a line of customs and immigration officials in between us and the SS *Stratheden*. I joined the queue of other passengers waiting to have their medical reports, passport, and visa checked. Holding back the tears with great difficulty, I said good bye to Kamalini and everyone else and proceeded to board the ship. A friend shouted, "Don't forget to write us!" I turned and gave him the thumbs-up sign. Saroj had promised to come to see me off, but I didn't spot her in the crowd.

Another student, Sheela Bildikar, was traveling with me on *Stratheden*. She had also been admitted to McGill for a PhD in mathematical statistics. Amongst a total of approximately two thousand passengers, there was a large contingent of students, about fourteen hundred of them, heading to the U.K., U.S.A. and Canada to study. They all conversed in Hindi, and during the voyage, it was my Hindi that improved, rather than my English.

The ship arrived at the Tilbury Docks near London on the afternoon on August 29. To my surprise, the tug boats that guided the *Stratheden* into the harbour were named *Dhulia* (the British name for Dhule, my native town) and *Nasik* (a city near Dhule). I hadn't expected to see such a connection to my hometown in a faraway place like London. I had a friend in the city who came to meet me after I disembarked. I stayed with him for three days, and he took me around to see tourist attractions in London including Big Ben, Tower Bridge, the Tower of London, and Madam Tussaud's Wax Museum.

Sheela and I were supposed to fly together to Montreal on September 2, but Sheela decided to stay in London for three more days and catch the flight on September 5. Our travel agent had advised us that we should reconfirm our flights to Montreal after arriving in London, anyway, so we went together to the British Overseas Airways Corporation office in London and presented our tickets to the agent at the counter. The agent put a sticker on Sheela's ticket noting the change, reconfirmed my flight, and handed back our tickets. On September 2, I arrived at the airport and presented my ticket and passport at the check-in counter. The agent checked my documents and looked at me with a question on her face. "The name on your ticket doesn't match the one on your passport," she said.

"What?" I was already exasperated by standing in the queue pulling along my bags.

"You're not Sheela Bildikar, are you?" She pointed to the name on the ticket.

I suddenly realized that the travel agent inadvertently handed Sheela's ticket to me and mine to Sheela. I explained the mix-up to the agent.

"I cannot issue you a boarding pass without a valid ticket," the agent said firmly, handing back my passport.

"Am I going to be stranded for a day? I asked, nervously clutching on to my passport.

"Let me check with my supervisor." The agent's smile gave me hope.

While the agent went looking for the supervisor, I was thinking about the complications this could cause. If I couldn't board the flight, I would have to go back into the city, exchange my ticket with Sheela's, have my flight changed, find accommodation in London for an extra night, make another trip to the airport, and send a telegram to McGill about my revised travel plans. All this would mean additional expense, which I could not afford. While these thoughts were rushing through my mind, the supervisor appeared on the scene. He checked the passenger list for September 5, and found Sheela's name on the list. Satisfied, he asked the agent to issue me a boarding pass.

After a six-hour flight, I arrived in Montreal at four o'clock in the afternoon. The weather was pleasant, with warm bright sunshine, just like in Mumbai. Two members of the International Students Association, Sunil and Suresh, met me at the airport. It was a half-hour drive from the airport to downtown Montreal. While we were passing through the downtown Suresh pointed to a big skyscraper on our left. "This is Place Ville

Marie, Montreal's first skyscraper; it will be inaugurated on September 13." That was a nice introduction to Montreal. Within few minutes we arrived at the apartment building on Durocher Street where GP was staying on the fifth floor. Suresh and Sunil helped me with my luggage up to the apartment. I thanked them both, while GP opened the door. Sunil gave me his address and asked me to contact him if I needed any help.

GP had invited another graduate student, Anil Sinha, to meet me. Over the next few days, Anil helped me find a room within walking distance, just half a block from McGill. It was on quiet Milton Avenue, which ended right at one of the side gates of the university. The apartment had a stove for cooking and a sink for washing dishes; I had to share a bathroom with one other renter. Though I arrived in new surroundings in a foreign country, everything was going smoothly. With so many fellow Indians around helping me, I did not even feel like I was in another country.

The day after I arrived, I made my way to the university and the mathematics department. I introduced myself to the secretary and she immediately informed Dr. Rosenthall, the head of the department of mathematics, about my arrival over the intercom. I was surprised when short, bald Dr. Rosenthall came out wearing a sports coat and took me into his office. In India, this kind of courtesy would have been unheard of. He asked about my journey and whether I'd managed to find accommodation. Then he asked his secretary Hilde to show me my office, which I was to share with two other students, including Sheela. On our way out, Hilde stopped by the mail room where there was a stack of mail boxes against a wall. "I have already assigned a mail box for you." She pointed to a mail box with my name on it. "Generally, the mail is delivered by nine and I sort it out into the mail boxes by nine thirty," she continued, giving me the key to my mail box.

Checking for mail around ten o'clock every day became my habit. About a week after my arrival in Montreal, I went to check the mail, though I was not expecting any. I was surprised to see a blue aerogramme from India. It was from Saroj. I was excited to see her name on the aerogramme. (The mail system in those days was very efficient; a letter from India could be delivered to Montreal in four days.) Standing in front of the mail boxes, I opened the letter. Saroj wrote, "I came all the way to Ballard Pier to see you off, but I missed the bus and by the time I arrived you had already boarded the ship. I didn't get an opportunity to say good bye to you. I hope you don't forget me."

I replied, asking how she could think that I would forget her. "Dear Saroj," I wrote, "Imagine the stress I was going through at the pier—more than seventy people came to see me off. There was a photo session. I wish you had been able to join us. I would have liked to see you in the photo."

Towards the end of March I received a letter from Kamalini announcing that our daughter had been born on March 21. "I have named her Shubhangi. I hope you like the name. She is as beautiful as her name signifies. I am looking forward to seeing you soon—please send the documents required for Canadian visas for both of us."

I wrote back, "I wish I was there with you to enjoy the birth of our daughter. I like the name "Shubhangi." You should apply for a passport for yourself with Shubhangi included on it. I will send the necessary documents for a Canadian visa as soon as you have received the passport."

The Canadian visa office needed a proof that my income would be enough to support Kamalini and Shubhangi. I approached the counsellor at the student aid office at McGill. He gave me a letter addressed to the visa office which indicated that my income would be enough to support Kamalini, but not a child as well. The visa officer only issued a visa to Kamalini. Kamalini was terribly disappointed and didn't know what to do next. We considered whether or not Kamalini should come to Canada without Shubhangi. It was a tough decision. Kamalini's mother offered to look after our seven-month-old daughter, but Kamalini was breast feeding Shubhangi. Accepting the offer meant switching Shubhangi to a bottle. It was a serious concern; but hoping for the best, we accepted her offer.

Kamalini arrived in Montreal on Wednesday, October 30, 1963. She wasn't fluent in English and she had trouble understanding the immigration officer's questions. The officer invited me to be an interpreter. Kamalini was twisting her hands, nervously standing in front of the officer's desk. He looked at Kamalini. She was confused about what was going on. "Do you have any gold jewelry to declare?"

"No," I answered.

"Mr. Wani, the question was for Mrs. Wani. Let her answer it. Just translate my questions into her language and then relay her answers back to me in English, please."

I was embarrassed, but the officer carried on as if nothing had happened. Satisfied with Kamalini's answers, he cleared her entry into Canada.

For the next three days, Kamalini was affected by jet lag. She was extremely tired after two long twenty-four-hour flights across several time zones. By Sunday, she was feeling refreshed and her sleep pattern had adjusted to Montreal time. That morning, Sheela phoned and asked if we would like to join her for some Indian grocery shopping. I asked Kamalini; she gladly agreed. It was a sunny day and the weather was mild. All three of us hopped on the bus to Enkins, the only store in Montreal in those days that carried Indian groceries. On the wall behind the cashier there was a Marathi poster promoting a famous mango pickle.

"Look at this," said Kamalini, beaming with surprise. "You told me that people here don't speak Marathi."

"They don't. The poster is just for show, Kamal. No customers here in the store except Sheela and us can read it." I stopped reading the information on the package I was holding in my hand.

"Then why did they put it up if people can't read it?" Kamalini insisted.

"It's just for ambience—to show they are selling a genuine product from India."

"I don't believe it." Kamalini said holding a jar of the mango pickle in her hand.

———————

Though her English communication skills were limited, Kamalini enjoyed life in Canada. She used to trample through the snow to the nearby superstore for grocery shopping by herself, uninhibited by the cold or potential language difficulties. There were six other graduate students from Maharashtra living around McGill, and three of them had their wives with them. Kamalini often met up with them to converse in Marathi. Though well-educated, they were all housewives; their visa status did not allow them to accept any employment in Canada. Once in a while Sheela would drop in to join us for meals.

Sometime in January 1964, we and half a dozen fellow students visited the Quebec Winter Carnival, the largest winter festival in the world, held in Quebec City. This was an opportunity to get a taste of French Canadian culture. Though McGill is located within the second largest French speaking city in the world, we were shielded from the general French culture; it seemed everyone in and around McGill communicated exclusively in English.

The weather was biting cold. Kamalini wasn't wearing thermals like the rest of us, only her heavy winter coat. While I was worried about her getting frostbite, Kamalini was totally unconcerned. We were all enjoying the sight of Bonhomme (the mascot of the carnival), a large snowman

sporting a red cap, black buttons and a ceinture fléchée—a wool sash—
tied around the waist. His huge, magnificent palace made of snow com-
pacted into enormous bricks was brilliantly lit up. All day, crowds danced
in front of the palace. We just watched them. We were too shy to join in
the dance, but we were impressed with the parades decorated with lights
and ice sculptures.

8

CHALLENGES AHEAD

As usual, I went to the office in the morning on Monday, June 1. It was a bright sunny day, hot and humid. None of my colleagues were in the office, so I wandered over to the department office to check my mailbox. There was a letter from Ram, Kamalini's brother. Still standing beside the wall of mailboxes, I tore it open, eager for some news about Shubhangi, already over a year old and perhaps already beginning to talk. Instead, Ram wrote that Shubhangi had died on May 27. There was no mention of the cause of death. I felt like crying, but held back my tears. I did not know how to convey the news to Kamalini. I walked back home with the letter in my pocket. I kept thinking about the student counsellor's letter to the visa office. Was my income really inadequate to support a child? Why hadn't the counsellor specified the extra amount I'd need to support Shubhangi? Perhaps I could have arranged to raise that amount.

Still consumed with these questions, I arrived home, slowly unlocked the door, and walked in. Kamalini was sitting on the sofa watching TV. When I saw her I gave in and started crying.

"What happened?" asked Kamalini.

I had no words to say. I reached into my pocket and gave her the letter.

Kamalini read it and started quietly crying too. I sat down beside her and patted her on the back.

"I shouldn't have come to Canada without her," Kamalini sobbed, wiping tears from her eyes.

"How could we have foreseen the future?"

Kamalini suddenly grabbed the photo album from the drawer of the writing desk and showed me the photo taken at the Mumbai airport before she left for Canada. Kamalini, looking worried, was holding Shubhangi in her arms, and they were surrounded by her mother, brother and several other relatives.

"She looks so innocent and cute," I said wiping my tears.

"My mother held out her arms to Shubhangi and Shubhangi stretched her hands to go to my mother." Kamalini was still sobbing.

"It's my fault. I shouldn't have let you come without Shubhangi."

Kamalini was pregnant when we received this news and I worried that the distressing news might affect the pregnancy. I did my best to keep her happy, taking her around to visit friends, going for picnics in a nearby park. When I informed Kamalini's gynecologist about the loss of our second child and told him that we were concerned about Kamalini's current pregnancy, he said that everything looked normal; there was no cause for concern. On November 5, Kamalini delivered a baby girl at full term. We had to decide on a name to be entered on the birth certificate. Sheela happened to visit us in the hospital and she suggested Varsha, meaning rain showers, and also one of the six seasons in the Hindu calendar. We liked it—though totally Indian, it was easy to pronounce for westerners too.

———————

Though I had to study for two courses, I was able to find time to do my research in mathematical statistics. By the end of 1964, three of my research papers, jointly authored with GP, were published in reputable statistics journals and a fourth joint paper was accepted for publication by another. I was due to finish all my course requirements in August 1965, after which point McGill would have no responsibility to provide me with financial assistance.

In early February, a job advertisement on the department's notice board caught my attention. Lethbridge Junior College was looking for an assistant professor of mathematics. I sent my formal application to the college on March 3. To my surprise, within a week the college offered me an assistant professorship with an annual salary of eighty-six hundred dollars. Kamalini and I were both relieved at the idea that we wouldn't be scrambling for money once my scholarship ran out.

I did not respond to the offer immediately, and the college principal called me on March 15 to press me for an answer. I promised to get back to him within ten days. I wanted time to consult with GP, who was my PhD supervisor, as well as Dr. Rosenthall.

GP had just resigned from McGill to join the department of statistics at Pennsylvania State University. On his recommendation, Penn State had offered me a part-time instructorship for two semesters. GP was still in the process of moving, so I walked over to his apartment to discuss the two offers. There was a stack of packed boxes in one corner of the room; the room was empty otherwise.

"What's on your mind?" GP asked, putting a few last books into a box.

"I'd like to accept the college offer and then spend two summer vacations at Penn State with you to complete my thesis work."

He straightened up. "You should give your sole attention to completing your PhD."

"Penn State's only offering me twenty-seven hundred. I can't support my family on that."

"You came to Canada to obtain a PhD, not to make money," he remarked tersely.

I offered an alternative. "I'm willing to forgo the college offer if I get a reasonable stipend."

"The Penn State offer is what a graduate student typically gets."

I was mortified. "Let me think. I'm confused," I said, after a moment.

"There is nothing to think; your goal should be to complete a PhD," GP insisted once again.

I came home in a despondent state of mind. Looking at my dejected face Kamalini asked, "What happened?" After hearing about my conversation with GP she commented, "What's wrong with you getting a decent salary while doing a PhD? GP's approach is always 'My way or the highway,' but it doesn't mean he's always right."

"You're right." I sat down at the table. "Apart from a huge salary difference between the two offers; the one from Penn State is only for eight months while the one from the college, though initially for a year, could be extended beyond a year."

The next day I went to see Dr. Rosenthall and summarized what GP had said. He leaned forward in his chair. "Accept the college offer. It's extremely generous. Even a PhD holder fresh out of school can't expect more than six thousand."

"How will Professor Patil's resignation affect my status?" I asked anxiously.

Dr. Rosenthall smiled. "You're a McGill student. You won't be orphaned because of his resignation."

I nodded. "So what are my options?"

"You may continue under his supervision, if he is willing. If not, I'll assign you another supervisor."

Kamalini was waiting when I came home. "How was the meeting with Rosenthall?" she asked curiously.

"He can assign me a new supervisor if I decide to accept the college offer. I feel bad going against GP's advice."

Unlike me, Kamalini was not confused about the decision. "As your mentor, GP should let you decide what's best for you. I think you should accept the college offer."

"I agree. Tomorrow I shall send my acceptance to the college." Changing the subject, I continued, "What's for dinner?"

"Nothing special—the usual rice, curry and chapatti."

In May 1965, Kamalini started to experience a breathlessness that deprived her of sleep at night. Her gynecologist referred her to Dr. Meakins, a chest specialist, who admitted Kamalini to hospital on June 8. He ordered chest X-rays and blood tests and diagnosed her with tropical eosinophilia, a condition resulting from an abnormal increase in white blood cells. Kamalini was discharged from the hospital on June 18, 1965. A few days later, we received bills from Dr. Meakins' office, the hospital, and the laboratories. When I added up the bills the total cost was almost twice my monthly stipend from McGill. While we were at his office for a follow-up visit I asked Dr. Meakins to give us an extension on paying his bill.

"Why do you need the extension?" he asked. He looked puzzled.

"I don't have any health insurance. I have to personally cover all the expenses."

"How are you going to pay, even if I give you an extension?"

"I don't have any savings, but I have a job beginning in September. I'll make regular payments every month from my salary."

Dr. Meakins began tearing apart the bill I'd brought with me. "That's too much of a strain on you. I'll waive my fees and request that the laboratory reduce their charges by fifty percent." He dropped the scraps of paper into the wastebasket.

"Thank you, Dr. Meakins. This is a great help." Kamalini and I were both delighted.

Dr. Meakins called his secretary and asked her to cancel his bill and then phoned the laboratory and requested that they reduce their fees. He also phoned the hospital's accounts department. They would not cancel their fees, so Dr. Meakins requested that I be allowed to pay the three hundred seventy-five dollar bill after I got settled in my first job. The accounts department agreed. Dr. Meakins then discussed Kamalini's recovery status with us. His treatment totally cured Kamalini's tropical eosinophilia, and she never suffered from it again.

––––––––––––

Without having to worry about Kamalini's health, we left Montreal in the last week of July 1965 and traveled to Lethbridge, Alberta, more than thirty-five hundred kilometres away. Instead of flying, we decided to take the Canadian Pacific Railway's glamorous transcontinental train, *The Canadian*, which featured a lounge and dining cars and an observation dome from which one could see in all directions. Whenever we would tire of sitting in the compartment, we would sit in the observation dome and watch the fleeting landscape. On the way, we stopped in Ottawa, Toronto, and Niagara Falls for sightseeing. Mr. and Mrs. Deans of the Kiwanis Club of Niagara Falls hosted us for two days and took us to see Niagara Falls and other sightseeing attractions around it. We were on our own in Ottawa and Toronto.

––––––––––––

I started work on September 1, 1965. The Lethbridge faculty was truly international. Like me, many of my colleagues were immigrants from different countries—India, Pakistan, Korea, Japan, Taiwan, Egypt, and the USA. Dr. Muhammad Alikhan from Pakistan was already well settled;

he had even bought a house. He took me to a townhouse complex called Rideau Court across the road from his home. I was intrigued by the name since Canada's Governor General's palace is called Rideau Hall. Kamalini and I decided to rent a two-storey townhouse with living areas on the main floor and two bedrooms on the upper floor—spacious compared to our tiny one-bedroom apartment in Montreal.

I was assigned to teach two courses, one in mathematics and the other in statistics. Realizing that some students were too shy to ask questions in the class, in my very first lecture I encouraged them to come and see me if they had any difficulties. Many students took advantage of my offer and we established a good rapport; two of them regularly came to me for help. Like me, many of the professors had an accent, but the students didn't mind since these dedicated immigrant professors also made themselves available for assistance outside of classroom hours.

With the onset of winter, temperatures dropped very low, and Lethbridge's high winds made it feel even chillier. Waiting at the bus stop in the cold became unbearable. Kamalini and I decided to buy our first car in October. I knew nothing about cars, and I sought help from another colleague whose landlord was a salesman in a car dealership for General Motors. As for the car, we needed a compact one. There was only one available; we didn't have a choice. Luckily it was blue, a colour we liked. The salesman helped us arrange for financing. It was the first time we had ever borrowed money from a bank.

———————

Right after our arrival in Lethbridge, Kamalini missed her regular period and we needed to consult a family doctor. We found one in a nearby commercial complex. We were taken aback when he confirmed that Kamalini was pregnant again. Apparently while hospitalized in Montreal, Kamalini had missed her birth control pills. We were not ready for another child, but we willingly accepted it. Neither space nor money was an issue, though we would have liked Varsha to be at least three before having a sibling for her.

Though the due date was in early April 1966, Kamalini experienced contractions and labor pains seven months into the pregnancy, and on February 16 in the early morning, she asked me to take her to the hospital as soon as possible. I put Varsha in her car seat, drove to the hospital, saw Kamalini admitted, and returned home to feed Varsha. At twelve-thirty, when I had just finished feeding Varsha, the hospital called to say that Kamalini had delivered a baby girl just after noon. The nurse mentioned that, being so premature, she would have to be kept in an incubator until she started gaining weight. In the end, it was six weeks before we could bring her home from the hospital; nevertheless, we called her "Sulabha," which means that which is easily obtained.

———————

When Sulabha was finally discharged from the hospital, Varsha came down with measles. Our family doctor warned us that measles are highly contagious and he cautioned us to keep Sulabha away from Varsha. Heeding the advice of the doctor, Kamalini and I divided our responsibilities. We kept Varsha and Sulabha in separate rooms. I took it upon myself to exclusively care for Varsha while Kamalini looked after Sulabha. Our precautions paid off and Sulabha did not catch measles.

———————

In April, the college renewed my contract with a revised salary that did not take into account my research or the number of papers I'd published in scientific journals since beginning my assistant professorship. Reluctantly, I applied for jobs at three universities, two of which offered better salaries and better working conditions that wouldn't be available in a junior college. I accepted the offer from Saint Mary's University in Halifax. The university was developing a mathematics department almost from scratch. It was an excellent chance for me to help develop new programs, particularly in statistics, which was my area of specialization.

In between my teaching schedule, whenever I could get time, I had been working on research for my thesis. I already had published four papers. The 1965 summer vacation gave me four months of uninterrupted time to work, and I prepared a fifth paper, which unified special cases discussed in my four published papers into a single theorem. My new supervisor had difficulty understanding it. He insisted that he could prove a stronger theorem and wrote a paper that got published in the *Canadian Mathematical Bulletin*. I noticed a serious flaw in his paper; the proof of his main theorem started with an assumption that was exactly what had to be proved. I revised my paper to include a discussion on the flaw with an example that invalidated every theorem my supervisor had "proved." The discussion added weight to my paper, and it was published in *Proceedings of the Cambridge Philosophical Society.*

After this fiasco, my supervisor did not feel he could evaluate my research and advised me to get GP's approval on the draft of my thesis. This defeated the whole purpose of having a new supervisor, so I wrote to Dr. Rosenthall and explained what had happened as modestly as possible. He wrote back: "You no longer have to consult Professor Patil about your thesis." I was delighted with Dr. Rosenthall's response. In November 1966 my supervisor accepted his error and cleared the way for my thesis submission. On February 20 I traveled to Montreal to make an oral defence.

"You achieved your goal for coming to Canada! I'm so happy," Kamalini told me when I returned from Montreal.

"McGill will mail my diploma about a month after convocation," I said, unpacking my bag.

"Aren't you attending the convocation?"

"No, I never attended for my previous degrees. I got them delivered by mail."

"This is the last one though. I want to see you receive your diploma at the convocation."Kamalini came forward and patted me on the back.

"Oh, Kamal, it's a hassle—line up to pick up the gowns, stand in line for at least an hour, watch hundreds of other people receive their diploma, and the process goes on."

"This is a once in a lifetime event! I don't want to give you a choice."

I grinned. "OK, you win."

9

THE DESTINATION

Now that I had completed my Ph.D. we decided to make a family visit to India. On June 17, 1967, we left Halifax and arrived in Mumbai on the 19th. My parents and my brother Chandrakant came to meet us at the airport. After five years, they were all excited to see us. Varsha, less than three, and Sulabha, just turned one, were delighted with the attention they were suddenly receiving, but they were reluctant to be picked up by any of the relatives. My brother Chandrakant stretched out his hands to pick up Sulabha, but she refused and hid behind me.

A few days after we arrived in Dhule, my parents organized a get-together of our relatives, friends and my former school teachers to celebrate our homecoming. This brought in invitations for speaking engagements which included, amongst others, one from my high school, three from colleges in and around Dhule, and many from local community groups.

When I began to explain the Canadian education system at one school, the children posed some interesting questions. One earnest little boy asked, "Do students in Canada cheat on their exams?" Cheating on exams is an endemic problem in India even now. In 1967, there had recently been violent attacks on supervising teachers who caught students copying answers. Apparently one high school student had placed a knife on his desk before beginning his exam in a blatant attempt to intimidate the invigilator. For the children I was speaking to, this kind of event was commonplace. Another boy asked, "Do Canadian teachers take revenge on the students who ask awkward questions?" Both students and teachers giggled at his question, but they were surprised when I told them that student-teacher relationships in Canada were very informal and friendly.

I often started my lecture to community groups by comparing Canada and India, citing similarities and differences and then providing few specific examples. I used to narrate a story about buying a coconut from a supermarket in Halifax. I bought one and it turned out to be rotten. A few days later I was shopping for another coconut in the same store. The store attendant, who was replenishing the vegetable stock on the shelf, casually asked me what I was looking for. I told him about the rotten coconut I had purchased the week before. To my surprise, he gave me a replacement without asking for any further details—he even cracked open two coconuts to find a good one. Such a scenario in India, at least at that time, was unheard of.

When we got back to Halifax I became engrossed in writing the textbook for a first course in mathematical statistics. In March 1968, I completed my manuscript, *Probability and Statistical Inference*, and New York publisher Appleton, Century and Crofts accepted it for publication. I expected the dean to recommend a salary increase on account of the textbook, but he did not. Perhaps he held something against me since I had resisted his interference in my grading of a mathematics course. There was no point in appealing to him. I confidently appealed directly to the president of the university, who not only upheld my appeal, but also promoted me to Associate Professor beginning in September 1968.

We were renting a two-bedroom apartment on the twentieth floor of a twenty-one-storey high rise called Park Victoria. It was a quiet, secure building, and our apartment was spacious with a nice view of the city. Four-year-old Varsha started going to a playschool located in the basement of the building. One morning I was getting her ready for school. I couldn't find her story book. I was looking around under the couch for it when I heard Varsha say "Fuck off; it was here on the couch."

I was shocked; looking into her face I asked, "Where did you learn this word, Varsha?"

"My teacher says it when she's angry," Varsha innocently responded.

I was concerned. One day, I decided to discuss the matter face to face with the teacher. I took Varsha along and entered the elevator. The elevator stopped at the twelfth floor and an elderly lady wearing red jacket carrying a matching purse got into the elevator. She smiled and introduced herself.

"I am Anne Boutilier. I teach at the playschool in the basement."

"I am Jagan Wani. This is my daughter Varsha. I'm actually taking her to playschool now. Is she in your class?"

"No, she must be in the other class." She was smiling at Varsha, trying to catch her eye. "Hello there."

Abruptly I said, "Is it possible to have her transferred to your class?"

She kept trying to engage Varsha, who was hiding behind me. "Hi, Varsha! Would you like to join my class?" Varsha didn't answer, just burrowed further into the corner of the elevator. Mrs. Boutilier turned to me. "I would be very happy to have her in my class."

All three of us walked to Varsha's classroom. Mrs. Boutilier stepped through the crowd of shouting and crying children and spoke to the teacher who was yelling at them. She had no objection to Varsha being transferred to Mrs. Boutilier's class, and my problem was luckily solved without having to confront her. After that day, Varsha attended playschool with the other class. Mrs. Boutilier treated Varsha like her granddaughter.

––––––––––

In April 1966 I had applied for a job at the University of Calgary, but my application was not even acknowledged. Two years later in December 1968 I was surprised to receive a letter from the U of C asking if I "might still be interested in coming to Calgary." The U of C definitely offered better opportunities, including a graduate program with 600 full-time students enrolled. Within a week, without even a formal interview, they offered me a job as associate professor of statistics.

––––––––––

Friday, May 30, 1969 was our last day in Halifax. As usual, Mrs. Boutilier took Varsha to playschool in the morning. I went to the university, cleared out my office and handed over the room keys to the office clerk. When I came home around noon, Kamalini and Sulabha were ready to go pick up Varsha. Mrs. Boutilier's class was at the playground. I walked up to Mrs. Boutilier and said, "We came to say goodbye to you." Kamalini and Sulabha followed me. Mrs. Boutilier called out to Varsha who was playing with other kids. She came running to us.

"I'll miss Varsha. She is such a sweet child." Mrs. Boutilier's voice wavered. "I can't bear the thought of her going away." Tears began running down her cheeks. "I'm sorry; I'm embarrassing myself."

"No need to feel embarrassed. We know your love for Varsha." I said, wiping my own eyes.

Mrs. Boutilier turned to Varsha, opened a gift box, and pulled out a gold chain. "Varsha, I'll miss you. Here's something to remind you of your days in playschool with me." She put the necklace around Varsha's neck and gave her a tight hug. It was a beautiful necklace. Varsha jumped up and kissed her teacher. Then, embarrassed, she ran over to show us her gift.

We walked home with heavy hearts. Kamalini commented, "I'll truly miss Mrs. Boutilier. She was like a mother to me." Four year old Varsha was happy, playing with the necklace. Three year old Sulabha was quietly walking with Kamalini, holding her hand. That evening, we left Halifax.

In Calgary we rented a two-bedroom apartment on the top floor of a seventeen-storey building within walking distance of the university. Several other professors, including five others from India, lived in the same building. We had a spectacular view of downtown from our balcony, and we were right across the street from the football stadium—home (as we were soon informed) of the Calgary Stampeders.

The majority of Indians in Calgary were either faculty members or graduate students at the U of C. There were no Indian grocery stores or Indian restaurants in town in the early seventies, but the India Students Association used to screen Indian movies in a lecture theatre at the university. Once we all went to watch one of these movies. Varsha and Sulabha, not knowing the language, were completely uninterested and began pestering us to go home. The association secretary kindly offered to look after them, but they refused to go with him. We thanked the secretary and left for home.

In the spring of 1970, Kamalini realized she was pregnant again. Though the due date was in early December, on October 3 she woke me up in the middle of the night and asked me to take her to the hospital. Varsha and

Sulabha were fast asleep. Without disturbing them, I drove Kamalini to the hospital, got her admitted, and returned home as quickly as I could. Around nine o'clock I got a call from the hospital saying that Kamalini had delivered a baby boy. He weighed only five pounds and four ounces. At eleven o'clock I took Varsha and Sulabha to the hospital to see their little brother. They were delighted to see him, but disappointed that they couldn't touch him; he was in an incubator. The pediatrician wanted him there until he started to gain weight. Kamalini was disappointed that she could not breastfeed him.

My grandmother had built a temple for Lord Rama, also known as Shreeram, the central figure in the Hindu epic Ramayana. To respect the devotion of my grandmother to Lord Rama, Kamalini and I decided to name the baby boy Shreeram. (Later we started calling him "Raju", a popular nickname with Indians.)

Kamalini and I had decided to limit our family to five, no matter the gender of the new baby, but we were both happy that Varsha and Sulabha had a brother. Raju was in the incubator for three weeks before his pediatrician discharged him on October 24. Varsha and Sulabha were thrilled, since they could now touch him and play with him. Varsha's favourite was peekaboo; Sulabha preferred to sing "this little piggy". Both wanted him to grip their fingers. Both would be around as helpers to Kamalini when she gave him a bath.

After coming home, Kamalini wrote to her mother to tell her about Raju's birth. She was overjoyed and wanted to see Raju. Kamalini was also longing to see her mother.

One evening after supper we were chatting around the dinner table. "Let's go to India this summer; I would like our relatives to meet Raju," Kamalini suggested excitedly.

I expressed my concern. "Raju will not be even a year old; the summer heat in India will not be good for him."

"What about the following summer?" Kamalini was eating quickly, shovelling food into her mouth.

"That will work better," I said. "As a matter of fact, should we consider returning to India for good?"

"I never thought about it," Kamalini casually answered.

"You know my desire to help the less fortunate in India. There are many desperate people who are neglected by the community—deserted women, isolated tribal communities, the mentally challenged..." I trailed off.

"What's your plan?" Kamalini asked curiously.

"Enroll Varsha and Sulabha in a girls' boarding school for two years, and once they adjust to Indian schooling, we can all return to India."

"I don't like the idea." Kamalini's voice was firm.

"OK, let's decide after we visit some schools. If you don't like it, we'll cancel the plan. But we should give it a try."

While planning for our India trip I received a letter from Saroj. At the age of thirty-six, she was getting married. Marriage opportunities had eluded her since she was twenty-two. Her mother used to tell me how she tried to arrange a marriage for Saroj. Every time, the prospective groom turned out to be a huge mismatch. Frustrated, Saroj told her mother not to bother. Now she was engaged to a man from a well-known but conservative and traditional family. Saroj hoped that Kamalini and I would come with the children for the celebrations, but I had accepted to teach a summer session course which was due to start soon after we returned from India, on July 3, the same day as the wedding.

———————

We'd booked our journey to Delhi via Rome on Alitalia airlines. While we were in the departure lounge waiting to board the plane for Delhi, Varsha and Sulabha were playing with Raju and Kamalini was watching them. Three other Indians, bearded and wearing red turbans, were standing nearby. They had been on the same flight as ours from Toronto to Rome. The elder amongst them mentioned that he was teaching mathematics at a college in Ontario. He was taking advantage of the summer vacation to travel with his two sons to New Delhi and from there on to Punjab, his native province. Somehow the conversation turned to the meal service on Alitalia flights.

"We're disappointed," the father commented.

"What happened?" I asked

Behind him, his sons grimaced. "They don't provide any vegetarian meals."

"They do, if you order at least three days in advance. We got vegetarian meals."

"We didn't know this," he said regretfully.

Just then we heard the boarding announcement. The trio rushed ahead of us and I saw the father talking to the hostess at the entrance of the plane. The hostess nodded her head. After about two hours, they started the meal service.

"What would you like, chicken or beef?" asked the flight attendant.

I leaned over Varsha from my middle seat and said, "We ordered vegetarian meals."

"We don't have any left. Another family claimed them—are you sure you made the order on time?"

"We did! Do you have anything else?" I asked.

The hostess shook her head sympathetically. "I can give you some fruit."

We accepted one apple each.

When we landed in Delhi, the summer heat was unbearable. The children were so uncomfortable that we decided to go straight to my home town; Kamalini and the children could stay with her relatives, and I would return to Delhi later to visit the school. We went to the Indian Airlines office. "We need tickets to Mumbai." I told the agent at the counter, showing him a demand draft payable to myself.

The agent looked down at the paper in my hand. "We don't accept demand drafts."

"My bank told me I could cash it by showing my passport."

"Sorry, we have a policy. You could go to a bank and get cash."

I looked at the clock on the wall. "The banks are all closed."

"I'm sorry, I can't help. Come back tomorrow with cash."

This simply wouldn't have happened in Canada. We had friends in Mumbai but none in Delhi. I was about to break down in tears. Why would I have wanted to return to India?

A man dressed in a light-coloured suit, purchasing his ticket from the next counter, overheard our conversation. "What's the problem?" he asked me.

"They won't accept my demand draft as payment."

"Let me see the draft." He held out his hand. "I don't see any problem. I'll give you cash—just sign the back of the draft."

"Thanks. You took a burden off my shoulders," I said. I handed the money to the agent and took the airline tickets. I turned back to the man.

"You came like an angel just in time. I don't know what I would have done."

"I just happened to have enough cash." He ducked his head.

We exchanged information about each other. I told him about my university job; he introduced himself as Badrinarayan Barwale, CEO of a company that supplied seeds to farmers. He gave me his card and I kept in touch with him for many years after that.

After arriving in Dhule's familiar environment, Kamalini and the children were happy that the weather was far better than the scorching heat in Delhi. After spending a day with my parents they all went to see Kamalini's mother, and I left for Delhi to visit a renowned girls' school. I had to pass through Mumbai on the way, which gave me an opportunity to visit Saroj. She happily took me to her fiancé's house and introduced me to his family, though I couldn't meet him as he was out of town on business.

The school and the dormitories were located on a large campus which also included a technical institute. Classes were out of session for the summer. In the morning on the day of my arrival I met the principal and told her that I was scouting out a school for my daughters. She took me on a tour of the campus. The school buildings were well maintained and the classrooms were tidy with educational charts hanging on the walls. Each room in the residence had four beds, with a writing table by the side of each bed. As we passed the technical institute building, she mentioned that her husband was the registrar there. "He informed the director about your visit." She smiled. "Actually, the director is interested in meeting you."

"I don't mind; when and where would he like to meet?"

"If it is convenient for you, he will meet you later this afternoon at my husband's office."

When I arrived at the registrar's office later that afternoon, the director was already waiting for me, dressed casually in a white shirt and dark pants. He stood up to shake hands with me and waved for me to take a seat. We discussed the purpose of my visit and my academic plans. I mentioned my desire to return to India after two years. The director clasped his hands over the desk. "Would you consider accepting a job in our institute?" Noticing the surprise on my face, he pressed on. "You eventually want to return to India, so why not take a two-year leave from your university, join us, and see how your daughters like it here?"

"I don't know if I can get leave."

Our conversation was interrupted by a phone call. I gathered from the registrar's side of the conversation that it was about a resigning faculty member who wanted a month's extension on vacating the apartment rented to him by the institute. The registrar was adamant that the extension not be granted and asked whoever was on the other end of the line to demand immediate possession of the apartment. I couldn't understand why a simple request to cover the transition from one place to another was being denied. Did I really want to return to India to work in such an environment? After the registrar got off the phone, the director turned to me and smiled, "I would be interested to know if your university does grant you a leave of absence."

"When I get back I'll check with the head of the department and let you know."

———————

Three weeks later we arrived at Mumbai airport to fly back to Calgary. The airline staff told us that the flight was cancelled, that they had rebooked us on a flight departing the following day, and that they had also made hotel arrangements. Having a full day at our disposal, we decided to visit a friend in Mumbai. After dinner, we returned to the hotel and got ready to leave. The taxi was waiting to take us to the airport when a young waiter from the hotel restaurant came rushing over to me. "Please sign the invoice for the evening meals, sir," he said, pretending to be polite.

"We didn't have dinner here."

"You are not paying it personally, sir." He grinned slightly. "We collect it from the airline."

"Doesn't matter who pays. How can I sign for something I didn't buy?" I protested.

"Your taxi is waiting. You don't want to be late for your flight, sir." He waved the paper at me.

There was no time to argue. I signed the invoice.

———————

The flight left on time, and two hours later we were served our pre-requested vegetarian meals. The children fell asleep as soon as they'd finished eating. Kamalini was in a relaxed mood.

"Are you happy with our India trip?" I asked her.

She stretched in her seat. "I was happy to see my mother. The other relatives were nice but lukewarm."

"Nothing was as pleasant as it was during our first family visit." I looked at her.

"I feel the same way. Do you still want to return to India for good?"

"I keep thinking about the director of the technical institute offering me a job; but then I also got a glimpse of the work environment in the institute. The registrar was adamant in not giving a month's extension for vacating quarters to a faculty member who had resigned."

Kamalini nodded. "I know. In a way, whatever happened was a lesson."

"You're right. I don't think there's any point in considering returning to India for good." I looked at Kamalini again.

She seemed delighted. She laughed. "I totally agree."

10

ACROSS THE OCEANS

Saroj always found time to share news with me. At the end of January 1975, while I was still learning to cope with the fallout of Kamalini's diagnosis, Saroj wrote to tell me that her mother had died. I was sad that I would never see Saroj's mother again. I recalled Mawashi's smiling welcome, and the potato curry she had cooked for me. Saroj wrote that Mawashi had always admired me.

During my India visit the following summer, I visited Saroj and then her sister Aruna in Mumbai. I sat down across from Aruna at the dining table in the kitchen. Aruna poured tea for both of us and we exchanged memories of Mawashi during my visits.

"You never knew the depth of Mom's admiration for you," Aruna said, stirring sugar into her tea.

I was embarrassed. "Of course, you would know it better than me."

Aruna looked me in the eye. "Mom would have liked Saroj to marry you."

"Really?" I was shaking my head, but Aruna was nodding. "What happened?"

"She wanted approval from Saroj." Aruna shrugged.

"Saroj objected?"

"Saroj worried that your parents were too conservative and traditional and you might decline. She didn't want to lose her friendship with you."

"I wish she had just accepted Mawashi's suggestion." I felt happy about all this information Aruna was unfolding before me. I wondered why Saroj thought she had to worry about my traditional parents, without giving me a chance to express my views on the matter.

"I think she overthought it. Hers is not a happy marriage." Aruna looked down.

"What do you mean?"

"More than once Saroj wanted to walk out of her marriage because she could not bear serious differences with her husband."

"What kind of differences?" I asked.

"Her in-laws want Saroj to be a housewife. For them a daughter-in-law working outside of the home isn't dignified," Aruna said.

"I'm sad, Aruna." I felt sorry for Saroj. It suddenly seemed that all her decisions in finding a life partner were based on misconceptions.

"Saroj should have listened to my mother. Your parents would have been upset, but their anger would have lasted for only a year or two."

"And life would have been far better for both of us."

Aruna raised her eyebrows. "You aren't enjoying your married life?"

I shared the details of Kamalini's schizophrenia—her weird behaviour, her disorientation, her abusive language—and the divorce solution suggested by the psychiatrist.

Aruna searched my face. "You're so cool and calm, Jagannath." She sighed. "I admire your patience."

———————

Though I was settled in Canada, balancing the challenges of dealing with my wife's schizophrenia and my academic responsibility at the university, India was still very much on my mind. In May 1975, along with two Canadians and five South Asians, I formed a society for Indian classical music. I envisioned the direct participation of non-Indians, not only in consuming and enjoying but also in organizing, learning and performing traditional Indian classical music in Canada. To signal this broad vision, Professor Gregory Levin, a non-Indian American, was made the founding president of the newly formed Raga-Mala Music Society. Our stated object was "to promote a better understanding and appreciation of Western classical music among the people of Indian origin, and of Indian music among other Canadians."

The CBC took note of this outward-looking approach and produced an hour-long radio program that included interviews with the founders, performances by the students learning Indian classical music, and interviews with their teachers and Dr. Ruari Mackenzie—the president of Raga-Mala at the time. The program was broadcast coast to coast more than once. After each broadcast I received a few congratulatory phone calls from my Indian-music-loving friends from all across.

Within a year of the formation of Raga-Mala, and with a bank balance of just two hundred and sixty-five dollars, we hosted a concert by the legendary sitar player Pundit Ravi Shankar. The estimated cost of the concert was six thousand dollars and we needed three thousand dollars of working capital. Six of the executive members ventured to be the guarantors to the bank. The concert was a grand success and helped in launching organizations like Raga-Mala in six other Canadian cities— Edmonton, Saskatoon, Toronto, Thunder Bay, Winnipeg and Vancouver. Locally, the membership in Raga-Mala grew threefold. Today, after more than four decades, Raga-Mala is still a flourishing society regularly staging performances of Indian classical music and dances by renowned artists from India as well as from North America.

***

My longing to help the less fortunate dates back to my school days. When I was in grade nine, I was running night classes for farm labourers to stop the exploitation of these labourers on account of their illiteracy. Though I had been in Canada for more than ten years, the desire to help the poor in India was still haunting me, but I began to think too of the many Indo-Canadians born and raised in India.

Three of my friends with varied professional backgrounds had similar hopes—Chintamani Adkar, an engineer from Montreal; Sunil Choubal, a radiation safety officer from Saskatoon; and Vinayak Gokhale, an architect from Toronto. We decided to meet in Toronto in August 1984 to discuss a course of action. Due to prior commitments, Sunil could not join us. The three of us met in Vinayak's home. Chintamani drove from Montreal with his wife Teja. I took a flight from Calgary. Along with Teja, Vinayak's wife Pratibha also joined the discussion.

"India paid for a major part of our education," I began. "We should pay back this debt."

"How do you think we can do that? Reimbursing the government of India would not be right," Vinayak said.

"It can take the form of assistance to the less privileged in India," I suggested, "for that we could register a charity so that our donors will receive tax benefits."

"Yes, the benefits could be Canada's contribution to our repayment plan," Teja pointed out.

"With our limited resources, we could only realistically assist social work in Maharashtra, yes?" Chintamani looked around the group. "I suggest naming our charity the Maharashtra Seva Samiti Organization, which we can abbreviate as MSSO."

We all agreed. Registering the MSSO was a simple procedure, but getting approval as charity was a challenge. After back and forth correspondence over a year, the MSSO received charity status in October 1985.

Later, for approved international development projects, Alberta provided a one-to-one match on MSSO donations, and Canada provided a one-to-one match on the amount that had already been doubled by the Alberta Government. In the process, our donation amounts grew fourfold.

Sometime in April 1990 a friend sent me a paper clipping describing the first-ever public meeting on schizophrenia held in Pune. It was so well-attended, according to the clipping, that the audience overflowed the auditorium into the hallways. Right away, I sat down and wrote a letter to the organizer, congratulated her, and asked her if she would be interested in helping me in forming a self-help group in Pune. I did not receive any response.

Later that year Aruna wrote to give me the sad news of Saroj's death. I had become aware of her health problems when I saw her, after many years, in 1986; she'd just been released from the hospital after being treated for a sudden heart problem, which turned out to be a false alarm. Aruna wrote, "In June 1987, Saroj was diagnosed with breast cancer and had an operation. The operation had to be followed by chemotherapy, but Saroj dreaded the side effects and declined further treatment. She pushed on for three years before she lost her battle on September 11."

I grieved as I read the letter. Our friendship of thirty-three years came to an abrupt end. I lost one of my caring friends. The best I could do was exchange memories of her in conversations with Aruna whenever I visited India. I still miss her during my India visits.

The Calgary chapter of the SSA was well established, so in 1991 I decided to leave my position in the SSA to focus on raising funds for the MSSO.

Two years later, I was surprised by a phone call from Joan Nuckles, a fellow volunteer from the SSA.

Joan was a caregiver to her son, Randy, who suffered from schizophrenia. She'd joined the SSA a year after it was registered. I used to support Joan in dealing with her personal trauma, passing on information on the psychiatrists I encountered and connecting her to other caregivers. She was a strong-willed person, able to care for Randy all by herself, but from time to time I would inquire about Randy, his treatment, his psychiatrist and so on. When she assumed the position of president of the Calgary chapter of the SSA, I helped her with fundraising, offering ideas and help in her new duties. Joan was a prolific writer who used to write for the local newspaper on mental illness. In one article she mentioned my support as "the most important kindness that was ever done" for her. She continued, "Dr. Jagan Wani changed my life and this in turn changed the life of my son. He saved us both."

We chatted for a few minutes, catching up, and then she said, "Jagan, the SSA has created an Honorary Life Membership to recognize outstanding contributions. I need your formal consent to nominate you for the award." I had no reason to decline; I willingly accepted her offer.

―――――――――

In June 1993, Vasant Bapat, a well-known Marathi poet from India, stayed with us for three days. Though Kamalini's mental health had improved a lot since May 1980 under the treatment of Dr. Roxburgh, there were still occasional hiccups. In November 1991, he had switched to injections of Fluspirilene, also known as IMAP. Unfortunately in spite of regular IMAP injections, Kamalini's condition lapsed a few days before the arrival of Mr. Bapat. During his visit, Kamalini did not leave our bedroom, but Mr. Bapat took it in stride with enormous compassion for Kamalini. On the second day of his visit, I took him to Banff National Park. Around noon we stopped at McDonald's for lunch. Munching on French fries, he asked me a question.

"Some believe that people with schizophrenia have split personalities, like Dr. Jekyll and Mr. Hyde. What's your opinion?"

"It isn't true." I thought for a moment, slurping my strawberry milkshake. "Consider an alcoholic: his behaviour when sober is so different from when he is intoxicated. We do not label this a split personality. The same is true for schizophrenia patients. Their behaviour is different under different circumstances—when the illness is under control and when it is not."

Just a month after this, Kamalini's illness was back under control and she came out of her shell. She offered me help with my social work and I put her to work stuffing envelopes with the two hundred fundraising letters I had to mail out. That July, our friend Raja Deshpande was terminally ill with cardiac complications. When I went to visit him, Kamalini came along with me to the hospital.

When we arrived, Raja was lying in bed wearing a hospital gown. He moaned and turned around to see us, too frail to raise his hand to wave us to our seats. His unfinished hospital meal was on a tray by the bed.

"Kamal-tai, I'm tired of eating tasteless hospital food," he complained.

"What would you like?" Kamalini moved closer to him to hear him more clearly.

"Pithale and chapatti," Raja whispered.

"Oh, that's simple." She smiled. "I'll bring it tomorrow."

The next day, Kamalini cooked pithale, a special Marathi dish made with spicy chickpea flour, and chapatti, an Indian flatbread. Raja could not sit up and eat with his hands, so I offered to feed him by cutting the chapatti into pieces and dipping them into the pithale. He thought this would be too messy. "Roll up the chapatti into a funnel and put pithale in the roll," he said.

Kamalini followed his suggestion and I fed him the rolled chapatti. When he finished, he tried to turn his head toward Kamalini, who was sitting at the corner of his bed.

"That was a delicious treat, Kamal-tai!"

"Thanks, Raja! Let me know and I'll bring you more home cooked food."

"It is very kind of you. I'll phone you if I need anything."

Kamalini began packing the dishes up. She was smiling, but she looked concerned. It was so difficult for Raja to speak. "You need some rest, Raja. We'll leave and return again tomorrow."

"Raja will not make it through more than a couple of days," I said to Kamalini on our way to the parking lot.

"I hope he will pass without suffering," Kamalini said. When I looked over at her she was crying.

I decided to accept early retirement beginning September 1, 1995. I was sixty, five years younger than the usual retirement age at the U of C. My colleague, Marguerite Fenyvesi, assistant head of our department, came to my office to congratulate me.

"I want to plan a retirement party for you," said Marguerite excitedly. "What would you like as a retirement gift?" She laughed. "General tradition is a gold watch."

"I don't want a gift. Creating a scholarship would be a better idea."

"You are very generous, Jagan! I'll announce the idea in the department's next newsletter."

Marguerite invited Murray Fraser, the president and vice chancellor of the University, to address the retirement party. I learned later that along with an invitation letter to Dr. Fraser she'd enclosed a booklet documenting the work of the Maharashtra Seva Samiti Organization and mentioned my involvement with the Schizophrenia Society of Alberta.

On November 23, 1995, my colleagues, students and friends gathered for the party in the Blue Room at the U of C. Even though it was a Thursday afternoon, we were joined by a big contingent of local actuaries who'd taken time off from work. The actuaries screened a video called "The Future of the Actuary; the Actuary of the Future." The presence of so many actuaries and their thoughtful presentation was a real surprise for me.

Dr. Fraser talked passionately about my initiatives to improve the quality of education, particularly mentioning the actuarial science program and its expansion into a co-operative program. He applauded me for my social work and appreciated that instead of accepting a gift I'd asked the department to collect donations for a scholarship endowment. He asked Marguerite if she had already collected enough for the endowment. She called out, "I'm about a thousand dollars short!" Dr. Fraser donated a thousand dollars on the spot.

Sometime in 1992, the U of C associate vice-president, Dr. Titus Mathews invited me to his office to ask if I could offer any ideas for innovative international collaboration. I suggested a Term Abroad Program (TAP) for any U of C students interested in gaining intercultural experience while taking selected courses taught by distinguished Indian instructors at the University of Pune.

In September 1994, the first batch of twenty-five students left for Pune accompanied by an academic coordinator from U of C. Numerous problems propped up during that first year. There were many complaints, including one from a student who complained of sexual harassment. The appointed academic coordinator who was to resolve these issues had disappeared from the Pune campus. It was total chaos. The program for the next year was put on hold.

The International Centre was in charge of the TAP. They contacted me in late September 1995 and asked if I would accept the job of academic coordinator. It was an interesting assignment involving coordination with the U of C administration, the participating students, their local instructors in Pune, the administration of the University of Pune, the local contractor involved in meal arrangements, the residence management, and so on.

Since I had retired from the university, I didn't even need to ask for leave. The TAP courses were to start on January 12 and run until March 27, however, I could not leave Kamalini for three months, though her schizophrenia was under control with regular injections every three weeks. I discussed the offer with her.

"I would like to come along." Kamalini seemed excited. "Our children are grown up; they are on their own. Raju is twenty-five years old."

I nodded in agreement. "This will be like a vacation. You could spend lots of time with our relatives."

We discussed the plan with Dr. Roxburgh. He approved it and provided a supply of injections for the duration of our absence from Canada. While in India we just had to find a nurse to administer the injections.

We were given an apartment in the same residence where the students were staying. One day Kelly Smith came to me, depressed after having received news of the death of the daughter of a close friend, who was a single mother. I consoled Kelly as best as I could. Another student, Monica Skrukwa, told me that her boyfriend was jealous of her since he didn't get the opportunity she was enjoying in India.

For interaction between the TAP students and local students of the same age, I organized meetings with many different student bodies in and around Pune. A particularly interesting one was a college in the small town of Shirur, seventy kilometres northeast of Pune. The students at the college were divided into 16 groups of 40 students each with one TAP student assigned to each group for an informal chat. To everyone's surprise, the TAP students were mobbed by the local students and I had to "rescue" them from the barrage of requests for addresses. One TAP student said, "I felt like Michael Jackson."

Some of the students wanted to learn Indian music and dance; some wanted to get yoga lessons; others wanted to visit social and development projects. I connected them all with local experts. Monica Skrukwa wrote in her letter to the U of C International Centre, "I did love my tabla (Indian drums) lessons, and *Kathak* (North Indian dance) lessons were a huge lesson in Indian culture.... Also, 'Women in Development' was an awesome and extremely depressing course, which (however) taught me a ton."

Some of these students are still in touch with me twenty years later. James Lowndes, one of the TAP students, surprised me with an email in February 2015. He was trying to establish connections with all the other students in the 1996 TAP program. He wrote, "I fondly remember our first trip together to a restaurant in Pune, and then to an incredible musical performance."

While I was dealing with the TAP students, Kamalini was having a great time with our relatives. Without the responsibilities of cooking, washing, and cleaning, and without any stress from dealing with Sulabha, there were no triggers for her symptoms.

———————

My time in Pune offered me an opportunity to explore the possibility of starting a self-help group for patients with schizophrenia and their families. Sometime in 1995, Minal Dani, a clinical psychologist from Pune, contacted me to inquire about SSA activities in Calgary. I phoned her and explained my quest to start a self-help group in India.

"I'd definitely like to help," she said. "Dr. Neha Pande is also interested. She's the head of psychiatry at the Byramjee Jeejeebhoy Medical College in Pune."

In late January 1996, the three of us decided to meet at café Raviraj around ten o'clock on a Sunday morning. When I arrived at the café, the middle-aged Minal, dressed in light grey sari, was waiting at the entrance. "Dr. Pande will be here any minute," she said. It being Sunday, the café was bit crowded. Minal asked the waiter to find a quiet place away from the entrance and he showed us to a table in the far corner. While we were still talking to the waiter, Dr. Pande rushed in. "Sorry for being late, a last minute phone call held me up," she apologized.

We started our discussion enjoying upama and idly sambar that Minal had already ordered.

"I've been trying to start a self-help group in India for seven years," I began.

"The main problem is stigma," Dr. Pande said, gesturing for the waiter to bring her a glass of water. "I see schizophrenia patients and their care-givers every day, and most of them want to keep it a secret, but there may be few who would come forward."

"Stigma didn't get in the way of forming a self-help group in Canada. Here it seems to be a stumbling block." I looked at Dr. Pande.

"Do you know any caregivers who aren't worried about stigma who would join us?" Dr. Pande asked.

"I do have two friends, both caregivers, who would step forward. Could you find a few more?"

Dr. Pande frowned slightly. "I can't promise, but I'll try."

Minal added, "I can inquire with my clients who come in for counselling."

During my stay in India we put together a team of seven people, and in April 1997 we formally registered the Schizophrenia Awareness

Association (SAA) in Pune. It took only a few weeks for stigma to show its ugly face.

One of the founding members brought in by Dr. Pande was a retired civil surgeon in his late sixties named Dr. Sudhakar Shendarkar, a caregiver to his daughter. I was shocked when he told me about his daughter's reaction to his participation in the association. "By joining the founders group, you have publicized my illness," she had reprimanded him. "Do you realize what you've done? Now no one will be interested in marrying me." Discouraged, Dr. Shendarkar told me that though he was a founding member, he would not be able to participate in SAA activities. We lost a dedicated volunteer. He told me that he was at a loss, not knowing how to deal with his daughter's irrationality.

Though I had successfully registered the organization, I couldn't make it a vibrant body. Of the remaining six founders, three of us were not residents of Pune. The other three were professionals busy in their own careers. While struggling to make something happen, I heard about an unregistered self-help group called Ekalavya, run by five active members. I suggested that we merge Ekalavya into the SAA. The merged group, though genuinely interested and dedicated, was still not fully equipped to undertake the tasks needed to make the SAA an active and engaged organization. To feel established in its identity, the group needed its own space for an office and occasional meetings. The fund-raising was also a major problem.

In March 2000, I visited India again. One evening, Hari Athawale, a friend from my college days, invited me for supper. We had both been enthusiastic volunteers on campus involved with, among other groups, Dnyana Sadhana, the organization that led to my friendship with Saroj. Another friend, Yeshwant Oak, along with his wife, joined us for supper. The dinner table was piled with Maharashtrian dishes, including freshly squeezed mango pulp to go with fried puris (an unleavened deep-fried

Indian bread), batata wada (potato fritters), and of course, rice and curry—all prepared by Hari's wife Usha. Yeshwant was heaping praise on Usha's cooking when Hari interjected. "Usha prepared this specially for Jagannath who is visiting India after almost a year."

"Let's hear about your social work in India?" Usha turned to me, embarrassed about the compliments. I described the SAA's dilemma. "We have a good team of dedicated volunteers who are trying their best, but it isn't enough. We have to raise funds, build good media relations, and manage staff. No one in the team has the background to handle these issues."

To my surprise, both Hari and Yeshwant offered to help. Hari had retired few years before, after a successful administrative career in the banking sector in India and abroad. Yeshwant had lots of volunteer experience through his association with one of the Rotary Clubs in Pune. Like Hari, he had also retired from his construction business a few years back. Both of them joined the SAA board and started taking keen interest in the SAA activities. The first task the duo undertook was to find a rental space for the SAA office, which soon brought regularity to the weekly meetings of caregivers and patients.

In September 2002, I noticed an obvious need for a comprehensive Marathi book with factual information on schizophrenia. The media was only reinforcing misconceptions about the disease, suggesting that people with schizophrenia have multiple personalities, that they are violent, that most violent crimes are committed by people with mental illness, and that schizophrenia is caused by bad parenting. Superstitions, including an implicit faith in black magic and a belief that the mentally ill are possessed by evil spirits, also play a role in Indian society. In order to produce literature to clear up these misconceptions, we needed funds that the SAA simply did not have. To obtain the necessary funding, I successfully submitted a project proposal through the MSSO called "Schizophrenia—Awareness and Reintegration Issues" to the Canadian International Development Agency (CIDA) for matching funds. In addition to the publication of books on schizophrenia, I proposed production of a movie to help remove the stigma associated with mental illness, and the establishment of a daytime rehabilitation centre. We received the first instalment of the grant in March 2003.

For at least seven years, I'd struggled to find someone to translate *Living and Working with Schizophrenia* from English into Marathi. I contacted some psychologists with established writing skills who had written in local newspapers about the illness. They kept the book for months but never responded. I was desperate to produce a Marathi version. I contacted a journalist friend, Aparna Velankar, who had translated many English books into Marathi. Though she was too busy to take on the project herself, she put me in touch with Kalyani Gadgil, the secretary of a well-known Indian scientist, Dr. Jayant Naralikar. Kalyani had translated *Jewels in the Sky*, a book on basic astronomy and astrophysics for school children written by Vinay Pattanayak. I contacted her and sent her a copy of *Living and Working with Schizophrenia*. We arranged to meet the following week.

One evening in late April, Kalyani, a middle-aged woman dressed in business clothes, dropped in to see me at the SAA office. I made my pitch to her about the necessity of having a book that would explain schizophrenia to the general public and clear up misconceptions about the illness. When I finished, she said, "The subject is totally new for me. I know very little about the illness."

"Knowledge about schizophrenia is not crucial for translation." I could already hear myself pleading.

She shifted in her chair. "True, but I was very disturbed while reading the book. I want to stay away."

I wasn't sure how to respond. Finally I said, "I appreciate your dilemma. Why not meet Shirisha Sathe? She is a clinical psychologist and an advisor to the SAA. If you are comfortable with the idea of meeting some patients and their caregivers, Shirisha could arrange it. You might feel differently after meeting real people. It might help give schizophrenia a face."

A few days later, I met with Kalyani and Shirisha back in the SAA office. "I attended a meeting with a few patients and their caregivers," Kalyani said, looking just past me at a painting hanging on the wall in front. "It made me depressed. I wouldn't go back to any of those meetings."

"Kalyani," I said, leaning forward on the desk, "if meeting with these people bothers you so much, imagine what the caregivers go through. They face that situation day and night."

Shirisha came to my help. "I deal with schizophrenia patients every day. Their stories are not pleasant, but they feel more relaxed if someone listens to them."

Kalyani nodded. "Give me some time to think about it. Let's meet again next week."

A week later Kalyani and Shirisha came back. This time Kalyani looked much more relaxed. She sat down across the table from me. "I contemplated Shirisha's comment during our last meeting and realized that the patients need help," she said calmly. "There *is* a need to create awareness and remove misconceptions about the illness."

"It is also important to make the patients understand their illness and to give them ways to cope with it," I said, trying not to show my excitement.

"The caregivers Kalyani met are distressed," Shirisha said. "They don't know how to handle their patients. Our insensitive society makes their lives miserable." Shirisha said.

"Yes, I'm now convinced of the need for the book." Kalyani smiled.

"Thanks, Kalyani." I felt relief wash over me. "How long will you need to complete the translation?"

She thought for a minute and then said, "I'll give you the first draft in the first week of July."

By the middle of July, Shirisha had read the first draft and suggested a few edits. In August 2003 we published *Schizophrenia—Ek Navi Jaaniv*, the first Marathi book on the subject.

To everyone's surprise, the book received rave reviews. One review in the widely circulated Marathi newspaper *Loksatta* stated, "the lucky ones who are not schizophrenia patients will also benefit from this book." Booksellers began arriving at the SAA office to purchase copies on a cash basis, which is unusual in the bookselling business in India. Generally, publishers distribute copies to booksellers on a credit basis, but the SAA was not willing to provide credit to the booksellers and then to chase them to collect the money. It didn't matter; readers from all over Maharashtra ordered copies directly from the SAA, and within six months, the first printing of a thousand copies was sold out. We printed another thousand copies. They sold out within a year. Our grand success made it clear to us that caregivers in India had had no reliable literature in local languages on schizophrenia available to them until the publication of this book. After the SAA sold nearly another thousand copies from the third printing, Continental Prakashan, a major publisher in Pune, took interest in the book and brought out a thoroughly revised, expanded second edition.

11

WRONG TURNS ALL ALONG

"TAKE NOTICE that an application will be made on behalf of SULABHA WANI before the Presiding Justice in Chambers on Friday, the 2nd October, 1992, for the following relief: An Order directing that the Respondent provide lump sum maintenance in the sum of $2,000.00 and on-going maintenance to the Applicant in an amount that the Court deems fit pursuant to the provisions of the Maintenance Order Act, R.S.A. 1980, Chapter M-1."

This was the crux of the legal notice I received on September 29, 1992, from Sulabha's lawyer. Sulabha's action stunned me. I had supported her for twenty-six years, and had every intention of continuing to support her. I did whatever I could to help her. How could she claim to be "destitute?"

In February 1982, Sulabha was about to turn sixteen. A few days before her birthday, she started skipping classes. When the vice principal confronted her, she bluntly told him, "I'm going to be sixteen. Then I'll be responsible for my own actions and will just drop out." The very same day, without waiting for her to turn sixteen, the vice principal suspended her. Having nothing to do, Sulabha just stayed home. Most often, she closeted herself in her bedroom. At the dinner table, none of us talked about her suspension; having turned sixteen she considered herself responsible for her own actions.

Though Sulabha didn't have a job or any other source of income, one day she surprised Kamalini and me by presenting us with gifts. She'd bought Kamalini a round red jewelry box to keep bangles in, and me a cream-coloured marble die with neatly carved, small round holes on six faces, just like on a gambling die, to be used as a pen holder.

One Thursday about a month later, Kamalini was about to finish her lunch and Varsha was waiting for a ride to school. Sulabha came out of her bedroom and rushed down the stairs. I was waiting by the door to the garage along with Varsha. Sulabha stopped in front of me and declared, "I have a terrible stomach ache, I need to be taken to emergency immediately."

"Could you please tell me the nature of the pain?" I asked.

"I can't describe it," she responded. I did not suspect any serious problem, but I agreed to take her to the hospital. Kamalini was concerned and joined us in the car.

On way to the hospital I took a small detour and dropped off Varsha at her school. At the emergency room at the Foothills Hospital the nurse carried out the routine triage checkup—blood pressure, pulse, and so on. After half an hour the attending physician showed up. He talked to Sulabha about the kind of pain she was experiencing. The doctor turned to me and said "Based on Sulabha's response; it is most likely an aspirin overdose." Kamalini stared at him, her face drawn and washed out under the fluorescent lights.

"No, it is not." Sulabha was vehement, but the doctor gently ignored her. He instructed the nurse to administer the needed medication and left. After the nurse had gotten Sulabha to swallow the pills, she also left. Suddenly there were only three of us in the room. I felt tears stinging my eyes. Sulabha was lying in the hospital bed staring at the ceiling. I took a step towards her. "Sulabha, why did you do this?"

She maintained a stern, blank face and didn't say a word, turning her face to the wall. Standing awkwardly behind me, Kamalini was also silent. The next day the physician asked if I wanted any particular psychiatrist to see Sulabha. I became worried that another member of the family was in need of a psychiatrist. I suggested Dr. Peter Roxburgh, who was treating Kamalini. Immediately after seeing Sulabha in the psych ward the next day, Dr. Roxburgh called me. "Sulabha objected to being treated by me. She says she does not need psychiatric help."

"Doesn't a suicide attempt call for psychiatric intervention?" I asked.

"It does, but the patient has the right to refuse treatment."

I didn't know what to do. I recalled reading that schizophrenia runs in families. Though it occurs in one percent of the general population, the chances of inheriting schizophrenia are ten percent for people who have a first-degree relative with schizophrenia. The illness doesn't always manifest itself as schizophrenia, though. Schizophrenia seems to involve multiple genes. It is certainly possible to inherit only some of them and be affected in a different way.

On the sixth day of Sulabha's stay in the hospital, a nurse called from the psychiatry ward. Kamalini and I had just finished lunch and were chatting around the kitchen table. I picked up the phone from the kitchen counter. The nurse was asking if Sulabha had come home.

"No, was she supposed to?" I found myself wondering if Sulabha had found another way to commit suicide.

"She's left the hospital but she hasn't been discharged. We'll report her to the police as a missing person if we can't find her." I wondered, how could the police help?

"Thank you." I hung up the phone. When I explained what had happened to Kamalini, she looked worried, but didn't say a word.

An hour later I got a call from Mrs. Marshall, Sulabha's former sociology teacher. She said Sulabha was with her. I breathed a sigh of relief. Mrs. Marshal took Sulabha back to the hospital, had her discharged, and brought her home.

A month later, while helping Kamalini clear the dinner table after supper, I mentioned my two week visit to India to attend a professional conference in May. Kamalini was loading the dishwasher. She stopped with a dirty plate in her hand, looked at me and said, "How will I handle Sulabha while you're gone?

She was right.

"Is it possible to cancel your trip?" Kamalini started loading the dishwasher again.

I rinsed out a cloth and went back into the dining room to wipe the table, trying to think. "You know I can't. This is part of my university job."

"Aren't you concerned about my health?" she called.

I bit my tongue. "I am. Do you have any suggestions?"

"Can you take Sulabha with you to India?"

"It will be expensive but it's a solution." I came re-entered the kitchen and looked at her. She was fiddling nervously with the cap from the dishwasher detergent. "Your health is important," I assured her.

She looked at me delightedly. "Thank you. I'll have peace of mind now."

Sulabha was happy to come with me since she had nothing else to do. While in India, I had to take her to every place I visited. My brother Chandrakant was the only one who could have looked after her. However, it was not fair to ask for his help; I recalled the ordeal he had to go through for five months in dealing with Sulabha back in 1977. Though she stayed with me, she did not interact with anyone I met. Of course, the language was a problem—she did not speak the local language and most of our relatives did not speak English.

In September, Sulabha contacted the principal on her own and re-enrolled in school. She made friends with Sheila, one of her classmates, who began to spend time in our home on a regular basis. During the summer vacation, Sheila got a job in a retail store and opened a bank account to deposit her paycheques.

One night after school started again, I was in bed, half asleep, when I received a call from Sheila's father. He was upset. He said, "Sulabha withdrew two hundred and fifty dollars from Sheila's account."

"How?" I asked in disbelief.

"Sheila gave a duplicate ATM card to your daughter and also shared the password."

"I would suggest that Sheila register a complaint with the police," I said.

He sounded confused. "What are you suggesting?"

"In June, someone forged a signature and withdrew one hundred and fifty dollars from Sulabha's sister's account," I sighed. "A stranger would not have had all that information about the account or what her signature looks like. We've registered a police complaint."

Sheila's father hung up.

I was embarrassed. Instead of asking Sheila's father to register a complaint with the police, I should have asked for a meeting between four of us to resolve the issue once and for all.

This was not the first time Sulabha had stolen. When she was twelve she had been caught shoplifting lipstick at The Bay. The store called the police, who brought her home. I was out of town for a meeting so Kamalini had to face the situation alone. When I came home, Kamalini told me what had happened, but I did not get angry. I was too confused. Sulabha did not want to talk to me; she simply went upstairs to her room.

In October 1983, when Sulabha was in grade twelve, I received a call from the vice principal to discuss Sulabha's request to drop a social studies course. Her teacher had recommended that Sulabha stay in the course, and participate more in group assignments and discussions. Her guidance counsellor pointed out that Sulabha would not qualify for the advanced diploma if she dropped the course.

Sulabha was getting A's in other courses. The problem with this course was the group work. Getting along with people was Sulabha's main hurdle. Sulabha wanted her social studies teacher to change the way he was structuring the course. Unsurprisingly, the teacher refused. When the administration would not let her drop the course, she stopped attending classes, and was suspended for truancy.

To make up for the missed credits, Sulabha spent an additional semester in high school and graduated in January 1985 instead of June 1984—but when she did graduate she was awarded the Alexander Rutherford scholarship and the Northland Flowers Trophy for excellence in art. This was the first time I came to know that she included fine arts as one of the subjects for her high school diploma; she'd never shared her school work with anyone in the family. Whatever we came to know was by accident, through notices from the school vice principal. The only item of her artwork we ever saw was a beautiful macramé chandelier she hung in the family room.

One day after her graduation, when we were all sitting at the dinner table, Sulabha announced that she wanted to become a movie producer.

I wanted her to be realistic. I said, "Ok, you did score the highest marks in your art course, but you need much more than artistic talent to be a film producer."

"Like what?" she asked in irritated voice.

"A film producer has to coordinate a team of people."

She put down her fork. "What are you suggesting?"

"Managing a group is very challenging. You could do something in mathematics, maybe computer science or accounting. You had an almost perfect grade in the accounting course."

"Yeah, but I didn't like it."

"I gave my advice. The final decision is yours."

"I've decided to be a film producer." She smiled.

"Have you checked the U of C calendar?"

"They don't have anything. I want to go into film studies at UBC."

Sulabha secured admission to UBC and I drove her to Vancouver in September 1985. In 1987, she came home for her summer vacation. While in Calgary, she registered for a course in social studies at the U of C, which she did not complete. Shortly after returning to Vancouver, she dropped out of the program at UBC, saying her poor vision and allergies made it too difficult to continue.

I wondered. In spite of these very same problems Sulabha had done very well in her high school advanced diploma, securing a prestigious scholarship. How could these problems now be cause for quitting in the middle? Was she finding an excuse because she was scared of not getting straight "A"s in the courses she was pursuing at UBC? I had no answer.

Sulabha did have multiple medical problems. She'd had skin allergies and eczema since early childhood. In junior high her asthma attacks prevented her from participating in gym class. She had chest pain whenever she ran or played soccer. But getting Sulabha to a doctor was a nightmare. Once we took her to an allergy specialist. She only reluctantly came along with us, and while the doctor was examining her for eczema, she all of a sudden burst into a stream of swearing. The doctor refused to treat her. She'd had a vision problem since she was six, but refused to wear glasses. Her vision started deteriorating when she was in grade nine but she wouldn't cooperate with the ophthalmologist and I could not get her treated.

When she turned sixteen she took charge of her own medical problems. She changed allergy specialists at least four times and went through six general practitioners. She must have been treated by half a dozen eye specialists.

———————

After dropping out of UBC, Sulabha decided to stay in Vancouver. From September 1987 to October 1988, she worked as a nanny for a doctor couple. After losing the position, she moved into a furnished basement suite. Her landlord was a retired construction contractor. After moving in, Sulabha started asking for changes to be made to the suite. When the landlord could not accommodate her requests, she reported to the City of Vancouver that the basement suite was illegally built.

In the last week of February 1988 Kamalini and I both went to Vancouver to help Sulabha move into another place. During our three-day stay, the landlord and his wife invited us for coffee. We all sat down at the kitchen table. They were lovely people. While we were chatting, I noticed a big dog tied to a tree on the lawn.

"Why have you tied the dog? Is he vicious?" I asked, looking out the window.

"Oh no, he's very friendly."

"He must be. We're strangers and he never barked at us." Kamalini nodded.

"Sulabha told us to keep him tied up for your safety."

"Really? May I pet him?" Kamalini asked.

"By all means." Sipping her coffee, the landlord's wife encouraged Kamalini.

The dog was gentle. When Kamalini approached, he looked at her expecting to be petted and licked her hand. She patted him on his back.

Out of work, in November 1988, Sulabha started a six-week bank teller course that she asked me to pay for. I willingly paid, but the course did not lead to employment. In June 1989, she started working part-time in an allergy-relief store, but she lost that job within six months.

Though unemployed, Sulabha decided to stay in Vancouver. I had been in Canada for twenty-seven years, but I could not shake off the memory of my family supporting me financially until I completed my master's degree. In the same spirit, I continued to support Sulabha, hoping that it would allow her to focus on finding the right career. I even considered buying a condo in Vancouver for her, but she didn't like anything that we looked at. In the midst of our condo search, Sulabha did approve of an apartment that was available for rent. After supper on the last day of our visit, while the three of us were still sitting on the kitchen table, I began a discussion of Sulabha's finances.

"I'll pay your rent. How much do you think you'll need for other expenses?" I asked.

Looking at me, she said coolly, "Six hundred a month."

I raised my eyebrows. "That's rather high."

"Well, how much would you give?"

"About two hundred and fifty."

Banging the table, Sulabha stormed out and left the apartment. It was ten o'clock. Kamalini and I were not familiar with Vancouver and did not know any of her friends in the city, so we couldn't do anything except pray for her safety. We stayed awake worrying about her into the middle of the night. In the early hours of the morning, we heard her come in quietly and go straight to her bedroom. We breathed a sigh of relief and tried to catch up on our sleep before heading back to Calgary as planned. Before leaving, we left five post-dated cheques for rent on the dining table.

In October 1989, Sulabha was scheduled for a cornea transplant. The operation was on such short notice I could not travel to Vancouver to be with her. I asked a long-time friend, Asha Lohiya, to support Sulabha. Asha paid a surprise visit to Sulabha and gave her a ride home after she was discharged.

One evening towards the end of December, Sulabha called. When I answered the phone she was crying. She said, "The manager of the apartment complex is harassing me."

"What's the problem?"

"He comes in without any notice when I'm gone out and steals my clothes."

Sulabha had had problems with her previous landlord as well. However, that landlord had been decent, and this manager seemed to lack decency. Whatever her history, I had to help her.

I said to her, "Sulabha, you are a thousand kilometres away. How can I help?"

"Please do something."

I phoned Asha, who was a paralegal, and explained the situation. Asha wrote a letter to the manager stating that, by law, he could not enter Sulabha's suite without prior notice unless it was an emergency, and warning him that he would face legal action if he did not obey the law.

Her letter did put a stop to the manager's behaviour, but it was a stopgap solution to Sulabha's housing issues. Her lease was expiring at the end of February 1990 and Sulabha was begging me to let her return to Calgary, even though everyone else—her mother, brother, and sister—was totally against her coming home. Her outbursts had been a cause of great stress in the past. When she was home, she shared a bathroom with Varsha. Even though they had separate sinks, she always blamed Varsha for not keeping it clean. Instead of talking to her and negotiating, Sulabha always stormed through the house to complain to Kamalini.

In the last week of February, Kamalini and I drove to Vancouver to bring Sulabha back to Calgary. Upon our return, I employed Sulabha in my private real estate company at a thousand dollars per month. I hoped that she would learn some things about real estate development and make progress in that direction. However, my hope was out of place; Sulabha did not contribute much. I had to terminate her employment in September 1990 due to the economic downturn.

Since Sulabha had been employed for more than six months, she was entitled to monthly payments from the Unemployment Insurance Commission for a period of six months, or until she found employment. In order to better her chances of finding a job, the UIC paid for an eight-month training course for office assistants. As part of the course she was assigned an internship at the U of C. She complained that there were not enough opportunities for gaining worthwhile experience and quit the internship in the middle. She graduated from the course in November 1991 but failed to get a job.

From February 1990 until April 1992, while Sulabha was staying at home, I used to drive her to medical appointments to save her the hassle of taking public transportation. Quite often, after finishing my lecture at the university I had to rush home to give Sulabha a ride. Once in a while, a student would approach me with a question at the end of the lecture and I would be five or ten minutes late. Whenever this happened, Sulabha would scare Kamalini with her outbursts of anger. Kamalini could not handle this stress. It was enough to make her panic and she would beg me to be on time.

In April 1992, Sulabha, who was twenty-six years old at the time, walked out of the house without informing anyone in the family.

12

WANI VS. WANI

The original demand of two thousand dollars in the initial notice from Sulabha's lawyer was raised to three thousand dollars in a supplementary affidavit on November 19, 1992. The Maintenance Order Act traced its roots back to the Poor Relief Act passed in 1601 in Britain, but it was still on the books in Alberta and it required me, as the father of the destitute daughter, to "provide maintenance, including adequate food, clothing, medical aid and lodging for the child." Sulabha's claim also included airfare and taxi fare to see doctors in Vancouver when equally competent doctors were available in Calgary.

My lawyer, Louise Campbell, who was supposed to be a specialist in family law, should have taken the matter to trial as soon as Sulabha applied for the first interim order in October 1992. Instead, she fought one interim order after the other until December 1993. In frustration, I consulted Mark Brown, another lawyer, for a second opinion. On his advice, in late January Ms. Campbell started the process for taking the matter to trial. It was set to take place over five days starting September 26, 1994, two years after the lawsuit was initiated by Sulabha. Meanwhile, Ms. Campbell's legal fees climbed and climbed to almost thirteen thousand dollars, and I was besieged with interim orders to pay more than fifteen thousand dollars to Sulabha.

One day in November 1992, I was sitting on the carpet in my study reviewing the legal papers spread around me and pondering Sulabha's actions, wondering if some lawyer was advising her or if she had invented this solution on her own. I had no answers. Just about then Raju walked into the room. "Why do you look so depressed?"

I looked up at him. "How can I pay what Sulabha is demanding?"

"It's a large amount," he said sympathetically.

He sat down and started looking at the papers. He became serious after reading Sulabha's latest affidavit.

"What will be left for me and your mother after paying her three thousand dollars a month? Am I going to be a slave working all my life just to pay my daughter?" Then with lumps in my throat, I said, "I would not like to live as a slave for the rest of my life."

Raju tried to console me. "Dad, don't give up. I'll have a job after I graduate and I'll earn a decent salary. I'll help you."

On December 15, 1993, I was ordered to pay Sulabha two thousand dollars immediately and another two thousand dollars at the beginning of January 1994. I was not aware of this, however, since I was not present at the hearing, and Ms. Campbell took two weeks to inform me of the court order. In the meantime, the opposing lawyer had issued a summons to garnishee my salary and bank account to collect the payment. As soon as I found out about the garnishee I called Ms. Campbell, but she would not take my calls. I left several messages on her voice mail requesting her to call back. She never did. I was frustrated and embarrassed.

Fourteen days after the garnishee summons had been issued, Ms. Campbell wrote to the opposing lawyer: "Please be advised that due to heavy court obligations daily since December 16, 1993, and Christmas and illness this week, I have been unable to report to Dr. Wani on the court order until today." Of course, this was a redundant letter written at my cost at the rate of one hundred seventy-five dollars per hour. Later during the trial, she admitted her negligence before Justice Dixon, saying, "Some of that non-payment in the first year, sir, may have been my fault." I should have changed lawyers but I was naive. Sulabha changed lawyers at least four times during the court process.

When Kamalini and I were in Vancouver at the end of February 1990, Sulabha had pleaded with me to co-sign on her credit card application. I agreed and co-signed her application with the credit limit set at five hundred dollars. When I opened the November statement, jointly addressed to Sulabha and me, I was surprised to find that the credit limit was twenty-five hundred dollars. The bank had increased the credit limit without my approval. I immediately met with the bank manager, paid the balance and asked him to cancel the card. He confirmed in writing that the account had been closed effective November 27. However, Sulabha still had the card in her possession. Within four days, I received a call from the bank asking me to pay an outstanding balance of two thousand dollars on the card, apparently a cash advance. I told them I wasn't responsible for any transactions after November 27.

(In October 1993, the bank threatened to sue me for the two thousand dollars plus interest. I sent them a registered letter enclosing the written confirmation of the credit card cancellation. I never heard back from them again.)

Sulabha was extremely mad at me after I cancelled the credit card. She met with my accounts manager at the bank and the manager requested a meeting with me in early July 1993. I visited the bank in the middle of July. The bank manager received me with a grim face and offered me a seat in the chair opposite his. He had all my files out on the table. "Your daughter told me about her lawsuit against you."

I sat down. "Yes, she is seeking a maintenance order, claiming to be disabled."

He leaned back. "She's expecting a sizeable monthly payment."

"Well, she can expect what she wants. The court will decide."

"She's confident of winning. She said she wants you to be 'taken to the cleaners' in the end." The manager looked at me to gauge my reaction.

"What can I say?"

"She also wants to have the police arrest you."

"Wishful thinking, I would say." I laughed, but my stomach suddenly contracted nervously.

The manager remained sceptical. "I'll look again at the matter and contact you as soon as possible."

Sulabha had settled with the bank manager regarding who would grab which parts from my sinking ship. Later, in cross-examinations, Sulabha reported that when she told the bank manager that she was seeking a maintenance order from her father, he said, "If anything ever happens, we have the first right to collateral assets."

And Sulabha said, "Well, that's okay. I'll have the first right to his salary."

I had a loan for ninety-seven thousand dollars from the bank. It was fully secured through a mortgage, and I was making regular monthly payments and there was no default. But the bank manager was alarmed by Sulabha's statements. In the first week of August 1993, he sent me a letter demanding repayment of the entire amount.

So this was the first step in the process of being "taken to the cleaners." With faint hope, I approached Ramesh Aggarwal, a friend with a common interest in social work. Without any hesitation, Ramesh paid off the loan and got the mortgage transferred in his name. I don't know how I would have handled the situation without Ramesh's help. (Three years later, in May 1999, I sold the property for two hundred and forty thousand, at least one hundred thousand more than what I would have received in a fire sale. After the sale, I paid back the full amount of the mortgage to Ramesh, including interest.)

On the morning of September 26, 1994, I arrived at the courthouse and waited in the corridor. I tried to relax but couldn't. When my lawyer, Sulabha, and her lawyer all arrived, I greeted Sulabha but she ignored me. The two lawyers were having a conversation. I joined them by introducing myself to Sulabha's lawyer, Joseph Markey. Ms. Campbell didn't look very happy about my taking the initiative to greet the opposing side. The door of the courtroom opened at nine o'clock, and we all took our seats. As Justice Dixon entered the room from the adjoining chamber, we all stood up to recognize him.

Justice Dixon and the two lawyers discussed the preliminaries, and then Sulabha was called to the stand to provide her testimony. Her statements were full of lies. While she was being cross-examined, Sulabha said, "My father continuously hit me, especially when I was crying." Ms. Campbell, in turn, asked Dr. Marilyn Lee—whom Justice Dixon referred to as Sulabha's "shoulder to cry on"—"Of the ten years that Ms. Wani has been your patient, she's lived in her parents' home for about six. Do you have anything on file that would indicate specific complaints of abuse?"

Dr. Lee answered hesitantly. "No physical abuse, but she describes emotional abuse due to discrimination regarding the way her brother and her sister were treated in relation to her."

"But just to clarify, no physical abuse during the time that you've been her physician?" Ms. Campbell wanted a straight answer.

"No. Not that I was aware of."

I came home exhausted that evening. Kamalini was anxiously waiting to hear how the proceedings had gone. Raju, Kamalini, and I sat down around the kitchen table. I told Kamalini that there had been no other testimony except Sulabha's and listed off the lies Sulabha had recited. Kamalini seemed hit hard, in particular by Sulabha's statement that "all three children treated her mother like shit."

"I would like to come to the court and tell the truth." Kamalini looked upset when she said this.

"It's not that simple, Kamal," I said, sipping orange juice Kamalini had poured for me.

"How come?"

"You can expose all the lies, but you'll be cross-examined by Sulabha's lawyer. It will create a lot of stress for you."

"Why not check with Dr. Roxburgh?" Kamalini picked up my empty glass and put it in the kitchen sink.

Before leaving for court the next day, I called Dr. Roxburgh. He strongly opposed the idea of Kamalini appearing as a witness, and wrote a note to the court stating that she should not be called as a witness as this would cause her mental illness to flare up.

On both the second and third days of the court hearing, Sulabha's witnesses gave their testimonies to help prove her disability. Sulabha's disability claim also required her to undergo both physical and psychiatric examinations, but she vehemently argued against the need for any psychiatric examination. The court rejected her arguments and ordered a psychiatric assessment.

Psychologist Dr. Thomas Dalby and psychiatrist Dr. Timothy Holden were the expert witnesses who examined Sulabha and testified at the trial. Both of them confirmed that Sulabha suffered from a somatoform disorder, described as the "unconscious translation of symptoms of psychological distress into physical disabilities." Based on the testimonies of the two experts, Justice Dixon concluded, "A somatoform disorder has subsumed her personality and her direction in life. Miss Wani refuses to recognize that she has psychological problems."

To explain Sulabha's behaviour, Dr. Dalby cited his observations on a widely-accepted MMPI-2 test. Based on the answers Sulabha provided in the test, Dr. Dalby classified Sulabha amongst "individuals who are rather immature, egocentric and selfish," but "present themselves as normal, responsible, and without fault" and "blame others for their difficulties and exploit social relationship to fulfill their own needs."

In their written reports, both Dr. Holden and Dr. Dalby discussed the reputed Canmore Pain Clinic, an interdisciplinary centre about a hundred kilometres from Calgary. They both felt that the clinic might provide a rehabilitation opportunity for Sulabha. Justice Dixon agreed. Under his orders, Sulabha underwent an evaluation at the clinic, and the staff assessing her prepared a comprehensive report.

Joseph Markey, Sulabha's lawyer, vehemently objected to including the report as a piece of evidence. Justice Dixon ruled him out but agreed to put Markey's objection on record. He then entered the report as evidence and invited Dr. Michael Mandel, one of the authors of the report, to be a court witness. Dr. Mandel's testimony cleared the air regarding the usefulness of the pain management program, the factors affecting its implementation in Sulabha's case, and the necessity of psychiatric treatment for her.

"Ms. Wani is suing her father for maintenance. Would that be a disincentive for the pain management program?" Mr. Markey asked.

"Well, obviously if she's no longer disabled, then the lawsuit would be over," Dr. Mandel replied.

Mr. Markey had no choice but to agree.

"In your report, you refer to the statement she made about deciding to make herself happy by pursuing what's right for her. How do you interpret it?" Justice Dixon asked Dr. Mandel.

"In pursuing this course, she's still very much playing the role of victim, rather than leaving it all behind and getting on with her life."

"Did you get the impression that she wanted to continue to be labeled as a disabled person?" Ms. Campbell asked.

"Yes, I would agree with that statement," Dr. Mandel said.

In his Reasons for Judgment, Justice Dixon accepted that Sulabha "experienced very serious illnesses over the years" and determined her to be a "destitute person who is not able to work," as per the Act. However, he wanted to examine the root cause of her destitution. He continued, "Is the child destitute for good cause? The good cause is not the simple ascertainment of physical disabilities and limitations affecting Miss Wani's capacity to find or succeed at work. There is a motivational or intent aspect that I need to assess in order to fairly address the overall claim."

To assess the motivational aspect, Justice Dixon considered a statement from the Canmore Pain Clinic report: "The members of the [Canmore Pain Clinic] team developed the impression that Miss Wani could at least be capable of some sort of part-time, sedentary work if she were appropriately motivated. It was suggested that her anticipated lifetime support serves as a large disincentive for returning to work." Mandel had also stated that "continuation in counselling, resumption of exercise and activities of daily living, and psychiatric treatment are seen as the most reasonable ways to assist this unfortunate woman." Justice Dixon accepted this recommendation and quoted the same in his final judgment.

Mr. Markey, who was very thorough in his presentation, stated in his written submission to the court: "This court must look not only at Dr. Wani's salary and income from other sources, but also at his assets in deciding the quantum of maintenance to be paid." He then provided the following point-by-point analysis of my financial affairs to the court:

On my professional development: "Dr. Wani is capable of earning an extra five thousand six hundred dollars per year teaching summer courses. He should use these earnings to look after his daughter rather than his research."

On my insurance: "His monthly payment of five hundred fifty-six dollars for life insurance is blatantly ludicrous and an outrageous waste of money."

On my expenses: "A mortgage payment of two thousand dollars per month to support a three hundred thousand dollar residence is exorbitant, and so also is three hundred dollars per month for electricity, water, and gas."

On my residence: "Dr. Wani is obviously going to have to sell his house."

On my retirement: "Why does he not want to work until age sixty-five? This is suspicious. He's still only sixty years of age and could work on a part-time basis to earn extra income to pay his daughter maintenance. His early retirement decision is nothing more than a ploy to appear to have less income."

Though his claims were ridiculous, I was uneasy about the effect they might have on the final judgment. Justice Dixon, however, rejected all of Markey's arguments.

Sulabha was not earning any money but was spending recklessly whatever she could grab from me or social services. Regarding her spending habits, Justice Dixon commented, "I'm dismayed to learn that Miss Wani's living expenditures averaged two thousand six hundred dollars per month between April and August of 1994. The multiple attendances for massages and chiropractic services, the home-care services, high laundry, high taxi costs, etc. simply cannot be justified."

In his decision Justice Dixon concluded, "This litigation is an uplifting experience for Miss Wani. She has studied the legislation, she discusses rules of evidence and asserts an unqualified right of maintenance. She sees the prosecution of this proceeding as a means of gaining control, through the court process, of the one person that she believes to have dominated her since childhood.... It is time for a wake-up call for Miss Wani and time to 'bury the hatchet' with her father and to get on with her life. I see appropriate counselling as a fundamental first start and I would suggest that Dr. Holden and Dr. Dalby be jointly asked to consider the nature and extent of same. I construe the Act as having limited application in limited circumstances and this is one such occasion."

Justice Dixon awarded Sulabha maintenance for only ten months at one thousand five hundred dollars per month, just enough to help her to put her life together. She never did follow through on his counselling suggestion.

In his Reasons for Judgment, Justice Dixon indicated that I could have challenged the legislation and requested a charter review of the Canadian Charter of Rights and Freedoms. Section 15 of the Charter reads: "Every individual is equal before and under the law and has the right to the equal protection and equal benefit of the law without discrimination." Since no other jurisdiction in Canada has a Maintenance Order Act similar to Alberta's, Justice Dixon noted, "The protections to or limitations that appear to be available to parents of children in most other common law jurisdictions in Canada appear not to be available to Alberta parents." This discrimination, Justice Dixon suggested, would have provided the basis for such a challenge. Ms. Campbell never pointed out the possibility of charter review. By her own admission, she didn't even know that basic Alberta Rules of Court that could have been used to handle the case.

The uniqueness of a lawsuit based on the obsolete Maintenance Order Act created waves in the media. On December 8, 1994, while the trial was in its concluding phase and the two lawyers were making their final pushes for their clients, an outsider walked into the room and started taking notes. The next day, the *Calgary Sun* carried the headline "Professor Target of Rarely Used Law." The news spread like a wildfire all across Canada and appeared in various newspapers under different headlines, from Saint John's to Vancouver. And the stories continued long after the trial ended. Justice Dixon took serious note of the Canada-wide publicity during trial and remarked, "This has been a very difficult case; certainly not an easy one for me to handle, particularly with the huge row that has now hit the front pages of the second section of the *Herald*."

The researcher for CTV's well-known public affairs program *W5*, Barbara Simon, contacted me in early May 1995 to let me know that *W5* was interested in the story on the lawsuit. I thought that appearing on the program might give me the chance to inform more people about the unfair Act that existed only in Alberta, but friends warned me that I would be asked questions that I might not be able to handle properly without legal counsel. I declined the offer to take part in the program.

Sulabha filed an appeal in March 1995 against the judgment of Justice Dixon. It did not cost her a penny, as Legal Aid paid all her fees. The appeal meant additional legal costs for me, however, as I needed a lawyer to handle the appeal. My expenses were mounting higher by the day. The total cost of the litigation, by the time a judgment was delivered in December 1994, exceeded one hundred and twenty thousand dollars, including legal fees, expert witness charges, monthly payments to Sulabha, etc. I had equity worth sixty thousand dollars in my residence but no bank would lend me any money against that equity because of the lawsuit. Once again, in the middle of the court proceedings, I approached Ramesh for financial assistance. He not only lent me the money, he also asked me not to tell anyone that he was helping me during that very difficult time in my life. I insisted that he register a claim for sixty thousand dollars against my residence as soon as possible, just in case Sulabha succeeded in taking me to the cleaners. He obliged. Five years later, in July 1999, I paid back all the money I owed Ramesh. Sulabha's dream remained unfulfilled only because of Ramesh's timely intervention.

I was not interested in retaining Ms. Campbell for the appeal. I contacted David Steele, a specialist in family law at Bennett Jones Verchere, a well-known law firm in Canada. He indicated that he would charge me on an hourly basis. "I've spent a huge amount on legal fees already and would like to cap the amount," I said to him. "The work involved with the appeal is limited and defined. Could we settle on a lump-sum amount?" He proposed a fixed fee of five thousand dollars to cover all legal matters up to and including the final judgment. I thought it was reasonable.

Mr. Steele assigned my file to James M. Petrie, who was interning with him. He prepared the defence under Mr. Steele's supervision and came up with very convincing arguments. The appeal was heard and dismissed on February 8, 1996. Of course, Sulabha was very angry. Shortly afterward, she changed her last name from Wani to Alai, Kamalini's maiden name.

After the trial Sulabha's landlord successfully sued her for nonpayment of rent, and in May 1995, the court ordered Sulabha to pay the arrears. The irony of the situation was that the trial was conducted with

Justice Dixon as the presiding judge and the order was signed by him. The only income Sulabha had was my support payment of fifteen hundred dollars a month. As part of the order, Justice Dixon directed me to deduct a monthly sum of three hundred dollars from the support payment and pay it directly to the landlord.

In July 1995, more than six months after the trial, Sulabha's massage therapist contacted me saying that she was unable to locate Sulabha, who owed her over four thousand dollars. I told her, "No one in our family knows her whereabouts. You may contact her through her lawyer, Mr. Joseph Markey." I don't know what course of action the therapist took.

Sulabha had no friends. Her friendship with Sheila had fallen apart after the ATM theft. She tried to get emotional support from Raju, and he did his best to help in her disputes with landlords and in finding a permanent solution to her accommodation problem, but she had no concern that Raju was in the midst of his final exams during the month of April. Fortunately, in spite of everything, Raju did very well in all his courses and completed the requirements for his bachelor's degree in commerce. In June 1994, a few days before the convocation ceremony, Raju and I were chatting at the dinner table after finishing supper. "I got a phone call from Sulabha," he told me.

"About?" I was intensely curious.

"She'd like to attend my convocation."

"You must be surprised."

"Yes, I am." He clenched his jaw. "After the havoc she created during my exams, I don't want her there. I told her no."

"It's your decision, Raju. She wants to maintain contact with you, but I do understand your feelings."

His voice softened. "Her presence would be very distressing for you."

I knew it was a difficult decision for him. A similar situation arose in 1998, before Raju's wedding. Sulabha wanted to attend the wedding, but this time, Raju did not have to make the decision on his own. Together, he and his fiancée Pratima decided not to invite Sulabha.

In August 1997, Kamalini and I were both served with a notice stating that Sulabha was going to sue us for sexual harassment. Since Legal Aid was not paying for this litigation, no action was taken on the matter for several years. In November 2003, her lawyer, Mark Freeman, withdrew from the case, and in March 2008, my lawyer filed the motion to dismiss the case due to lack of action for a period of five years. On August 5, 2008, the case was dismissed.

Currently there is no contact between Sulabha and anyone in the family. She kept in touch with her mother until November 2003, when she phoned Kamalini to tell her that she was leaving the country. Sulabha asked her not to call her anymore. Coincidentally, this was the same time her lawyer Mark Freeman unsuccessfully tried to find her home address so he could serve her a notice stating his intention to cease representing her. In his application to the court regarding being unable to personally serve the notice, he stated: "Our file indicates that the Plaintiff was homeless throughout our dealings with her."

I was heartbroken to see the label "homeless" attached to Sulabha.

13

"LET ME OUT"

We attended Raju's sister-in-law Priya's wedding in Saskatoon in May 1999. It was an eight hour drive covering seven hundred kilometres and Kamalini's schizophrenia symptoms were prominent. Kamalini felt that Raju's in-laws did not treat her with respect. She complained to me that according to Indian tradition, she being the mother of their son-in-law, they should have presented a special gift to her along with the invitation to Priya's wedding. I tried to convince her that traditions in Canada are different than those in India. She wouldn't buy my argument.

Kamalini could have stayed home, in view of the perceived disrespect from Raju's in-laws, but she decided to come anyway. The wedding was at the Saskatoon Inn, a popular location with the Indian community for holding major ceremonies. The hotel staff were familiar with the exact needs for Indian weddings—the specially catered Indian food and an appropriately decorated dais for performing the wedding rituals.

Close to four hundred guests were already sitting and watching the rituals: Kanyadan (the father giving away a most precious gift, his daughter, to the groom) followed by Saptapadi (the walking couple taking seven sacred vows, one vow per step, promising their commitment to a happy married life). These were performed under a decorated mandap, a canopied altar specially designed for the ceremony. The priest was explaining the meaning of each ritual in English. Kamalini paced restlessly up and down in the passage. Most of the guests were our acquaintances, aware of Kamalini's schizophrenia and able to ignore her. Those who weren't looked at her with irritation, but no one risked asking her to sit down in one place.

We were staying with a friend, Sunil Choubal. In between the wedding events we would return to his house. Kamalini isolated herself in the guest room. Though hungry, she refused to eat. The day after the wedding, we were having breakfast before heading back home. Sunil's wife, Sujata, had spread out a delicious breakfast—aloo paratha, upama, poha, and vada sambar, along with fresh fruit. Sujata and Sunil went into the guest room and unsuccessfully asked Kamalini to join us for breakfast. She simply didn't say a word in response to their request.

I chose not to join Kamalini in refusing to eat—I needed energy to drive back to Calgary. On such occasions, I always remembered the flight attendants' instructions on airplanes concerning the use of oxygen masks: always put on your own mask first before helping others. One elderly woman, who had attended the wedding and was also staying with Sunil, said to me, somewhat in a scolding voice, "How can you enjoy your breakfast when Kamalini is not eating? I don't feel comfortable eating if Kamalini is hungry."

"If you can persuade Kamalini to join us for breakfast, you'll perhaps do better than I could," I said to her.

The woman went to the guest room where Kamalini was lying on the bed. "Kamalini, I do not feel good eating breakfast without you. Please get up and join us." Kamalini didn't respond; apparently she turned on her side towards the wall, avoiding the woman. Satisfied with her attempt to persuade Kamalini, the woman then relished her breakfast.

Another couple joined us for our return journey to Calgary. During the drive, Kamalini, who hadn't eaten for three days, kept on rambling incoherently. "Stop the car," she screamed at one point. "Let me out, right here."

I was alarmed by her screaming. The couple in the backseat were stunned. We were in the middle of nowhere. On both sides of the road were acres and acres of bare farmland. There were no humans in sight. I ignored Kamalini's screaming, which was continuously escalating; I just kept on driving. After four hours we stopped for lunch. We tried to persuade Kamalini to have lunch with us, but she refused and stayed behind in the car.

When we got home late that night, she went to the living room and fell asleep on the sofa instantly. I didn't know what to do except to wait to see Dr. Roxburgh. At Kamalini's next appointment in June I explained the incident to him. He turned to Kamalini and asked her if she wanted to say something. "Don't ask me, ask him," Kamalini retorted, looking at me. Peter turned to me and smiled. "I have nothing to say." I said.

IMAP had been extremely effective for Kamalini. However, for reasons unknown, in June 1999 the drug manufacturer discontinued its production, and, unwillingly, Dr. Roxburgh switched Kamalini to flupentixol (also known as fluanxol), the closest equivalent of IMAP. In an attempt to moderate Kamalini's anger and incoherency, Peter increased the dose and called her every week instead of once every three weeks. After a few weeks, Kamalini stabilized and I heaved a sigh of relief.

In May 2008, Kamalini and I traveled to Boston to visit one of our friends. Kamalini was able to participate in conversations, play with the two children in the family, and generally enjoy the visit. She even came along on a shopping trip to buy gifts for the children. Our friends protested that they didn't need gifts, that our visit was a gift in itself. Kamalini smiled mischievously. "We are not buying gifts for you; these are for the children." After consulting with the children, Kamalini bought a bike for the boy and a Barbie for the girl.

We had planned to stop in Toronto on our way home to attend a Marathi drama festival. Many weeks before, I had booked advance tickets—seats in the centre of the front row. I didn't know why, but Kamalini's mood was off as soon as we landed at the Toronto airport. Our hosts, Vishwas and Devayani, received us at the airport and together we went to the festival venue. The visiting drama troupe from Maharashtra included some of the top actors and actresses from the Marathi theatre. I was looking forward to seeing a presentation of the two plays: Kabaddi Kabaddi was a new drama about sport, nationality and belonging, with a haunting love story at its heart. The other play, Natigoti, revolved around the dilemma of the mother of a mentally challenged son. Before the performance and during intermission, as our friends were exchanging greetings, Kamalini maintained her grim face, not saying a word. A friend, Asha Pawagi, invited us, along with our host couple, for dinner at her place following day.

The next evening, we started getting ready to leave.

"I am not coming," Kamalini announced.

"Why not?" Devayani asked in frustration.

"I just don't want to," Kamalini said, glaring at Devayani and then at me.

Devayani turned to me and Vishwas. "I can't leave Kamalini alone. I'll stay back with her. Asha specifically organized the dinner for Jagannath and she's invited other friends to meet him. So you both must go." Vishwas and I agreed with her and we left for dinner. On our arrival, Asha asked curiously, "Where are Kamalini and Devayani?" I explained the situation; Asha took it in stride. The other guests had seen Kamalini day before at the drama festival; they naturally wondered about her absence. Most of them were aware that she had schizophrenia; they expressed their concern. I began to feel oppressed. I thought to myself, "I must maintain a balance between caring for Kamalini and my other responsibilities. If I don't, I myself could go into a depression." With this thought in mind, I tried to socialize with all the guests and enjoyed the delicious dinner Asha had prepared—spiced rice, potato curry, a salad made of cucumber and carrots, and fruit salad for dessert.

Back at the house of Devayani and Vishwas, Kamalini had not eaten anything. Devayani could do nothing to persuade her. During the four-hour flight to Calgary the next day, Kamalini didn't say a word to me. As soon as the seat belt sign went off and the passengers started crowding in the passage, opening the overhead bins and taking out their carry-on bags and filing toward the exit, Kamalini, who had nothing to take out from the overhead bin, started walking fast to the front of the plane without waiting for me. In the crowd of passengers I lost sight of her. After looking around for a few minutes I proceeded to the airport exit, and was relieved to find her waiting near the exit. "Why didn't you wait for me? I was looking for you all over," I said. Without saying a word she walked with me to the airport exit.

Raju was waiting in the car to take us home. "How was your trip, Mom?" Raju asked. Kamalini ignored him and got into the car in silence. Raju looked at me. I nervously smiled.

The next week I accompanied her to the regular injection clinic. Dr. Roxburgh had retired from his psychiatry practice in 2003 and a new psychiatrist, Dr. Pamela Manning, had replaced him at the clinic. She'd continued using fluanxol, and when I explained the Kamalini's episode in Toronto to her, she increased Kamalini's dose. Things got back to normal within two weeks.

Over the years, Kamalini developed a good rapport with the nursing staff at the clinic. She communicated directly with them and arranged her visits to the clinic without my support. Whenever I traveled to India for extended periods, the nurse went beyond the call of duty and visited our house to give Kamalini her injections. If Kamalini was accompanying me on a trip to India, the clinic would give us medicine, syringes, needles, and written instructions.

In August 2013, however, Kamalini skipped a scheduled injection appointment. I decided to meet the psychiatrist to discuss Kamalini's refusal to go for injection. Realizing that she would have to have an injection one way or another, she quietly accompanied me. I did not have to say much to the psychiatrist. She increased Kamalini's dose again and Kamalini recovered; her hallucinations disappeared.

General practitioners, though the first point of contact for families encountering mental health issues, are often not equipped to handle these issues as effectively as they handle physical health issues. I brought up this matter in our meeting with the SAA's medical advisory board in March 2004. Dr. Devendra Shirole, a member of the board, acknowledged the situation. "The examination papers for the first medical degree contain very few questions on mental health," he told us. "Medical students usually do not even attempt these questions. They choose other options and still manage to get their degree with high scores."

I looked around the table and asked, "Is it possible to do anything to address this issue?"

"The Pune Psychiatrist Association could organize orientation sessions for GPs," Dr. Shirole responded positively. (Dr. Shirole was the President of the Pune Psychiatrist Association.) Under the guidance of Dr. Shirole, the SAA organized half-day orientation sessions on mental health for two groups of GPs. To reach out further, the SAA published a comprehensive book, Divided Mind—A Handbook of Schizophrenia, covering the topics included in the orientation program. It contained articles written by thirty-five experts in related areas, covering not only the allopathic system of medicine but also the ayurvedic and homeopathic systems, among others. Though the book was primarily aimed at GPs, judging from the sales records many others found it useful—including clinical psychologists, counsellors, support-group leaders, volunteers, students, patients, and caregivers. The first edition of the book was sold out within a year.

In 2007, the SAA teamed up with Continental Prakashan, a publishing house in Pune, and produced a series of translations of non-technical books relating to schizophrenia for the general public. These included *A Beautiful Mind*, the story of Nobel Laureate John Nash, and *Breaking Points*, the story of John Hinckley Jr., who tried to assassinate President Ronald Reagan in 1981.

A Beautiful Mind was released in 2001 and won the Oscar for Best Picture that year, bringing schizophrenia into the media spotlight and removing some of the stigma associated with the disease. The Hollywood movie, however, focused on the heroism of the brilliant mathematician John Nash. It did not provide guidance on how to accept and live with an incurable mental illness. The SAA felt a need to produce a movie with a main character who was not a hero like John Nash, but an ordinary person dealing with schizophrenia. We wanted the plot to include the struggle of the patient coming to terms with a lifelong illness, the frustration of the helpless caregivers in the family, and involvement with self-help groups.

With these ideas in mind, we approached Sumitra Bhave, known for producing socially-oriented Marathi movies. Since the project we'd proposed to CIDA included the production of a movie, the funding was not an issue. Sumitra came up with a script in which Shesh, a schizophrenia patient, is obsessed with a devrai (a sacred grove, a forest protected by the community in the name of God). Shesh's obsession for the devrai turns into a series of hallucinations and he starts personifying the forest in the form of a goddess.

The premier of *Devrai* for invited guests was held on June 14, 2004, in the main theatre of the National Film Archive of India in Pune. Seating was limited to three hundred thirty, but the theatre was filled to capacity. In the audience there were theatre owners, psychiatrists, patients, caregivers, and media representatives.

Prior to the screening of the movie, Sumitra addressed the audience. "I'm thankful to Dr. Wani and his colleagues at the SAA for giving us this opportunity to work on this subject! It was an enriching experience for the entire team... The feeling of compassion has risen in us—not only for the patients and caregivers but for all human beings!"

Atul Kulkarni, a well-known Marathi actor, played the role of Shesh. One film critic commented, "Atul's portrayal of a complex character—his body language, his mannerisms, his voice modulation and the entire personality of a mentally disturbed man—is simply outstanding." The audience would have loved to meet Atul. However, due to a prior shooting commitment he was not able to be present for the premiere. All the other actors and actresses were in attendance.

Many in the audience rushed to see me after the screening. Anil Damle, the owner of the Prabhat theatre in Pune, offered his theatre for a commercial screening as soon as we were ready for it. SAA volunteer Gurudatt Kundapurkar observed, "It was a soul-searching experience. Our teary eyes took a moment to recognize even the most familiar faces outside the auditorium."

A middle-aged lady approached me after the screening and introduced herself as Mrs. Vijaya Pendse, friends with SAA's president Yeshawant Oak.

"I wish this movie was available five years back," she said. "Our family's understanding of schizophrenia would have saved two lives."

"I'm so sorry!" I said.

"We didn't know how to handle my twenty-five year old daughter Vandana's schizophrenia. She jumped to her death, along with her daughter, from the terrace of a six-storey building."

I was devastated to hear this.

Later, Thomas W. Dodson of the Oregon Psychiatric Association watched the movie. He said, "It stands out because unlike other movies, such as *Shine* and *A Beautiful Mind*, the main character is not a superstar, but just an ordinary person like the majority of those affected with schizophrenia."

All in all *Devrai* won fourteen awards, including the ones received by Atul Kulkarni, at many national and international film festivals. The most prominent award was the silver medal presented by the President of India at the Indian Government's National Film Awards ceremony, the Indian equivalent to the American Academy Awards. The State Government of Maharashtra awarded a cash prize of sixty thousand dollars for winning the President's Silver Medal.

By selling the rights to ETV to screen the movie on their Marathi channel, we were able to make fifteen thousand dollars. India's ministry of external affairs paid another fifteen thousand dollars for copies of the movie with subtitles in French, English, Arabic, Russian and Spanish respectively. The addition of thirty thousand dollars brought the total revenue to ninety thousand dollars. The SAA invested the money in an endowment fund, and the interest from this endowment now helps the SAA to meet the shortfall in its annual operating expenses.

I acted as SAA president until March 31, 2004. I'd wanted to relinquish the position long before that, but my fellow executive members would not let me do so. Finally I decided to put my foot down. "I'm sixteen thousand kilometres away from the scene," I explained to them. "Yeshwant handles most of the local matters, which are the responsibility of the president, so it's unfair of me to hold on to the position. The SAA has achieved many milestones. Since Yeshwant is fulfilling the duties of the president in my absence, I recommend he be the president from now on."

In August 2004 I received an email from the Indian Psychiatric Society inviting me to attend the society's thirty-fifth annual conference in Pune as an honoured guest. The inaugural function was held on October 15 in the Bal Gandharva Auditorium, one of the largest conference halls in Pune. Besides the psychiatrists from different states in the West Zone, local caregivers, members of mental health organizations, and representatives of many pharmaceutical companies were in the audience. In my address I candidly covered my journey in facing Kamalini's schizophrenia, my experiences with half a dozen psychiatrists, and the formation of the awareness associations in both Canada and India. It appears that I struck the right chord; the audience appreciated my open attitude and the lack of stigma in my address. It was received with thunderous applause.

The organizers had arranged a screening of *Devrai* for the next day, which was followed by a discussion the audience enthusiastically participated in. After the screening, a person dressed in a dark business suit approached me. He gave me his card. "I am Nandkumar, Sr. General Manager of Sun Pharmaceutical Industries."

"Nice meeting you," I said.

"I am impressed with your movie. Would you consider screening it in other parts of the country?"

"Why not?" I laughed. "Only if we could get a sponsor though!"

He was serious. "We would consider sponsoring it, though the language is a problem. Your movie is in Marathi. In order to screen it all over India we need it in Hindi."

"Dubbing it in Hindi would require a sizeable investment," I said, "and we are a small organization depending on public donations for our day to day operations."

Nandkumar said that he would check with his managing director. I followed up the conversation with a formal letter to Nandkumar at Sun Pharmaceutical, but the sponsorship amount they eventually offered was not enough to pay for the dubbing costs.

Medication is an important aspect of schizophrenia treatment—but to make life worth living, medication needs to be supported by non-pharmaceutical therapies. Elyn Saks, the author of *The Center Cannot Hold*, writes, "While medication kept me alive, it had been psychoanalysis that had helped me find a life worth living." Similar views are held by many others who have survived their schizophrenia. There are a variety of supporting therapies to be used in conjunction with medication, including counselling, yoga and other physical exercises, breathing exercises, games, music, art, and painting.

Everyone on the SAA board agreed that if the SAA could have a rehab centre of its own, then it would offer these activities to patients and keep them engaged throughout the day. Families would get a few hours of respite to attend to other work, and patients would be able to overcome their feelings of loneliness as they became aware that there were others facing similar problems.

With financial assistance from the MSSO combined with matching funds from CIDA, the SAA was in a position to construct the much needed rehab centre in Pune. Yeshwant, as a retired construction contractor, offered to invite the bids from contractors, guide the SAA board members in selecting the right one, and supervise the construction. The SAA was lucky to find a piece of land with an adjoining open space located in Dhayari, a new suburb of Pune about twenty kilometres southwest of the city centre. The rehab centre was ready for occupancy in July 2006. Touchingly, Yeshwant suggested that the centre be named in honour of Kamalini. After all, it was Kamalini's schizophrenia that prompted me to become an activist for mental health.

Today, the *Kamalini Kruti Bhavan (Kamalini Activity Centre)*, spread over two floors with a total floor space of five thousand square feet, gets plenty of sunlight and fresh air; the open space has been developed into a garden with a playground. The centre attracts attention from patients and their caregivers in other cities, and some families of schizophrenia patients have relocated to Pune to take advantage of it.

———————————

Yeshwant continued as the president of the SAA until August 2010. He completed two major projects—the production of *Devrai* and the construction of the *Kamalini Kruti Bhavan*.As his wife's health deteriorated, he expressed his wish to retire from the position of president but offered to continue on the executive committee and provide guidance from time to time. I discussed the replacement options with him. He mentioned Amrit Bakhshy, a caregiver to his daughter Richa who suffers from schizophrenia.

Reading an article about the SAA's rehab centre in a newspaper, Amrit had convinced himself that it would be the right place to help Richa. He took early retirement from his well-paying executive position at an export house in Mumbai and in April 2007 moved to Pune and enrolled Richa at the *Kamalini Kruti Bhavan*. Since relocating to Pune, Amrit had been volunteering at the rehab centre. He was spending many hours there every day and helping the staff with administrative duties.

Recognizing Amrit's administrative background, his devotion to the SAA and his understanding of mental illness as a caregiver, I accepted Yeshwant's suggestion. We both discussed the matter with Amrit. He was pleasantly surprised with our proposal but was not sure how others in the Executive Committee would receive our recommendation, given that he had been with the SAA for only three years. I convinced him that it was the qualifications and not the seniority that mattered in this situation and assured him I would personally take on the task of persuading the executive committee. With my assurance, Amrit agreed to take on the role of the president. Amrit now devotes full time hours to SAA activities. He believes that he was never so busy in his professional life of forty years. His involvement has connected the SAA to many organizations at the national and international level. At the national level, besides serving as an advisor to many sister organizations, the most prestigious organization Mr. Bakhshy connects with is the National Institute of Mental Health and Neuroscience (NIMHANS), constituted by the Government of India under the NIMHANS Act. The government appointed him not only as a member of the policy committee of NIMHANS but also made him the chairman of the Hospital Management Committee. At the international level the SAA is one of the collaborating organizations for the World Health Organization-funded international diploma in mental health law and policy.

14

IT ALL BELONGS TO HIM

One day during the spring of 1979, Kamalini, Varsha, Raju, and I were on our way back to Calgary after spending a day in Banff National Park. I happened to look in the rear-view mirror and saw a dark blue van speeding towards us. As it got closer, I could tell it was not going to slow down. The driver of the van seemed to be dozing off. Suddenly he decided to overtake our car, but instead of passing us in the left lane, which was empty, he swerved into the right. As the van passed us it tilted, and its wheels rubbed against the protective steel guardrails lining the highway. I thought it was going to push our car into the left lane.

I didn't panic but everyone else in the car, though terrified, did not scream. The van's tires tore, and the friction between the steel rims of the van's wheels and the steel guardrail created a shower of sparks in front of the van. Unbelievably, I found myself enjoying the flying sparks. It was like watching a spectacular movie scene.

As the sparks flew, the van swerved in front of our car. In a split-second decision, I slammed on the brakes. The other driver lost control, and his van veered into the left lane in the opposite direction. I thought it was going to brush against our car, but instead, it circled behind us and came around our right side again. I increased my speed to avoid the possibility of a crash. The van grazed the right corner of the rear bumper of our car and finally stopped on a grassy strip in the middle of the divided highway.

It took me a minute to slow down. I stopped about a hundred metres from the scene and ran back to the van. There was not a shred of tire left on the front wheels. All I could see were bare steel rims. Miraculously, nothing serious had happened to the middle aged driver. He was seated in the driver's seat wearing a white-blue chequered patterned shirt. He showed no signs of shock or panic. There were only tiny black spots on his face from the flying sparks.

Looking straight at him, I asked in a calm voice, "Are you OK?" He sounded guilty. "I'm lucky to be alive."

"It certainly is a miracle. You totally lost control of your van."

"I am so sorry! I don't know how it happened. Are you all OK?" He peered around me to look at our car.

"We are all safe. Do you need any help? Shall I call the police or a tow truck?"

He shook his head. "Thanks for your offer. I'll manage it on my own."

As soon as I returned to our car, Varsha anxiously inquired about the driver of the van. "The driver seemed to be OK. He declined my offer of assistance." I said

"He was definitely driving irresponsibly," Varsha said. "The moron. The police would have given him a ticket, at least."

"We are lucky. Death had opened its jaws, but destiny intervened and saved us," Kamalini commented. It was the first thing she'd said.

Varsha grinned. "Daddy, you performed even better than a stuntman in a circus."

This escape from the jaws of the death was like the beginning of a second life for me. I decided to use it for bridging miles and minds across the oceans between India and Canada.

During my India visit in December 1974, I stopped by Dhule for a family visit. One day after having supper, Nana, my father, called a meeting of his children. He had just turned seventy-four. We, seven brothers and one sister, sat cross-legged in a semi-circle on the carpet in the living room facing Nana. The purpose of this meeting, he told us, was to distribute the estate he had inherited from our grandmother, Aai. Her portrait hung on the wall above and behind Nana, and it looked as if Aai was supervising the distribution process. The living room was painted red and white on the occasion of Diwali in November. The carpet had also been replaced; the new carpet was plush brown.

It had been more than twelve years since I left India. My youngest brother Gopal had been ten at the time. Though I frequently visited India, we had never had such a meeting. Now all brothers were adults; two were still pursuing college education for undergraduate degrees, one in commerce—B.Com—and the other in agriculture—B.Sc. (agri.); they all looked excited to get a share of the estate.

So many people cling to their worldly possessions until the last moments of their lives, and quite often, death signals the beginning of a family feud. I'm grateful that my father called this meeting a few years before his death to amicably distribute all his assets amongst us.

"I'm not looking for any share of the estate. I'm happily settled in Canada." I said at the beginning of the meeting.

"I appreciate your generosity; it will increase the share for all of us. But I suggest you accept your share and decide later how to use it," my brother Raghunath said. "Even if you don't want the money for yourself, you may want to use it for charity."

"Raghu is right, Jagan. Using your share for charity is a worthwhile idea," Nana said.

I looked at my father and said, "I accept your wish, Nana. But I don't want any share of the estate for my personal use."

My sister Pushpa, who had moved to the nearby town of Nagardeole after her marriage in 1963, had traveled to Dhule to attend the meeting. She turned to Nana. "You had to sell a good chunk of farmland in order to pay for my wedding expenses, including dowry. I consider that my share of the estate," she said.

We finally agreed to divide the assets into eight shares, all approximately equal in market value: one share for each of the seven brothers and one for Nana. We decided that my youngest brother should choose his share first, and I, being the eldest, would accept what remained after the rest had chosen their shares. Though I lived fifteen thousand kilometres away, Nana chose me to handle two additional responsibilities: one, to guard the share of my mentally challenged brother Suryakant, and second, to manage his own share with the understanding that I use it to provide for him and my mother during their lifetime.

I wanted to return the inherited assets to Nana, sooner or later, by supporting social projects for the benefit of the less fortunate in and around my hometown. In 1987, I used all my inherited assets to establish the K.S. Wani Memorial Trust in memory of my father, who died in 1982. Kamalini did not object to my donating the inherited assets for a social cause. One quality I'd always appreciated in Kamalini was that she never pestered me for expensive jewelry or fancy clothes. She insisted on living simply. With Kamalini's schizophrenia in remission, I had peace of mind to devote to furthering this new venture.

The Trust received significant assistance through Maharashtra Seva Samiti Organization (MSSO) I had established in 1984. In cooperation with the MSSO, using the matching funds mechanism available through the Provincial Government of Alberta and the Government of Canada, the Trust completed the construction of schools, hostels, hospital, and a rehabilitation centre for the mentally ill; it also established vocational training programs, and many similar projects. The beneficiaries included the tribal people, the mentally challenged, the hearing impaired, the physically challenged, destitute women, orphans, and the mentally ill. The Trust and MSSO both shared a common principle: "Give them a chance, not charity."

Over the period of thirty-two years, the MSSO remitted seven million dollars to India for the benefit of the under-privileged. The most noteworthy of the projects was the production of the schizophrenia awareness movie *Devrai*. Yeshwant Oak, then president of the Schizophrenia Awareness Association, proudly represented the SAA to receive the silver medal for the movie from the President of India.

The MSSO also wanted to encourage the second generation to contribute in helping the less fortunate in India. Under the aegis of the MSSO, to date more than twenty-four youth have provided volunteer services to MSSO partners in India. They've not only paid for their own travel costs but also raised funds for the NGO partners they visited in India.

———————

On June 28, 2009, my family and the MSSO celebrated in one stroke four milestones—my seventy-fifth birthday, our fiftieth wedding anniversary, the Silver Jubilee of the Maharashtra Seva Samiti Organization, and the book launch of my Marathi memoir, *Andharatil Prakashwata* (Lighted Pathways in the Dark). The celebration of the MSSO silver jubilee and the book launch was organized by the MSSO executives in the University Theatre at the U of C, and the birthday and wedding anniversary party was organized by family in the Alberta Hall at the U of C. Four major Indian NGOs supported by the MSSO came all the way from India to attend the celebrations. MSSO took this opportunity to recognize those who had significantly contributed in its growth—in particular David Oke, CIDA program officer, and Srinivas Pabbaraju, who audited the financial statements of the MSSO for decades without charging any fees.

It was the first week of December 2012. I had just finished my breakfast and was about to resume my daily routine—check my emails, catch up on MSSO matters, and start working on my writing projects. I was opening my laptop when the phone rang.

"I'm calling from the office of the Governor General. May I speak to Dr. Jagannath Wani?" said the person at the other end.

"Speaking," I said.

"You've been selected to receive the Order of Canada," the person announced.

I could hardly believe my ears. "This is the big surprise of the day," I responded.

She laughed. "Before making a public announcement we need to confirm that you will accept it."

"I'm delighted; I'll be happy to accept," I said.

"Please, do not announce this to anyone else until it is officially declared."

"I sure will not," I responded.

The announcement appeared in all newspapers and on TV channels on 30th December 2012. The investiture ceremony was held on May 3, 2013 at Rideau Hall, the official residence of the Governor General of Canada. I received the insignia at the hands of His Excellency the Right Honourable David Johnston. The citation included my academic contributions in the field of actuarial science, promotion of India's music and dance in Canada, advocacy of mental health, and service to India's destitute.

According to the Vedanta philosophy, life is divided into four phases, called ashramas. Each phase is twenty-five years, more or less, except the last one. The first twenty-five years are to be dedicated to education and learning while observing celibacy (brahmacharya), the next twenty-five to raising a family and looking after the household (grihastha), and the next twenty-five to living a detached life where you share your wisdom with others (vanprastha). If you live beyond seventy-five years, then you enter into the last phase—renunciation (sannyasa): complete withdrawal from all worldly responsibilities. Purely by coincidence, I got married at the age of twenty-five and established the MSSO at the age of fifty.

Entering the phase of renunciation at seventy-five was my deliberate decision. There are two different aspects to renunciation. The first is giving up worldly possessions. For many years now, I have been sharing whatever wealth I acquire.

The other aspect of renunciation involves giving up positions of responsibility. Everything, no doubt, has an end. One has to know when to stop; the timing of the end is crucial. Sometimes destiny makes the decision for you, but human greed can play a major role. It is appropriate to quit when everyone still wants you to stay. An old man with diminished vision, impaired hearing, and reduced energy levels becomes an object of ridicule if he clings to a position of power. I was fortunate enough to be able to give up my responsibilities on my own schedule.

I took early retirement at the age of sixty, and I did not cling to a position in any of the societies I created, with the exception of the MSSO. Since no willing volunteer offered to take on the responsibility, I was the president for twenty-six years, until 2009. The reins of the MSSO are now in the hands of a new team, but I do provide assistance if and when asked.

There is a famous quotation: "In this world nothing can be said to be certain, except death and taxes." Kamalini and I both have been affected by cancer. My colon cancer was detected in October 2012 and, except for metastatic spread to my lungs, was successfully operated on. Kamalini's was detected in October 2014 as metastatic growth perhaps resulting from a uterine cancer operation ten years earlier. She lost her battle to cancer on 30th December, 2016. Raju has always looked after all our medical and other needs diligently. Our grandchildren, Deliya and Saajan, like their father, have been a constant source of joy to both Kamalini and me.

I am now free from all major responsibilities in my professional and social life. I did not bring anything with me on my way into this world, and I will not carry anything on my way out. I am trying to live by the following words of Tukaram, the famous seventeenth-century saint poet from Maharashtra (which have been translated from Marathi):

> "Though I opened this treasure,
> it all belongs to Him
> I am just His porter
> Carrying this load for Him"

ACKNOWLEDGEMENTS

Madhukar Deshpande, Amrit Kumar Bakhshy, Chitra Phadke, Gayathri Ramprasad, my son Raju, and daughter-in-law Pratima all provided me with many suggestions to expand, delete, modify or reorganize parts of the manuscript. Their suggestions led to considerable improvements in the presentation of my narration.

A dozen writers in residence in and around Calgary provided critical comments on early drafts. Cathy Ostlere and Rachel Small provided editorial assistance and Lizzie Derksen edited the final version of the book. They all enhanced the quality of my manuscript.

Psychiatrists Kishore Saraf and Peter Roxburgh, and a friend, Mangala Wasudeo, verified and confirmed the authenticity of the matters relevant to them.

My consultant, Allen Zuk, promptly guided me in the publishing process of my book.

Asha Pawagi from Toronto, who loves reading, offered to read my first draft, chapter by chapter. She found the draft to be inspiring. Her comments assured me that the common reader would enjoy reading my book.

I am very thankful to all of those who contributed to the success of this project. They all share the merits of this book. Any shortcomings are reflections on my personal limitations and hence are my responsibility.

Calgary, Canada   Jagannath Wani
March 2, 2017   .   wani34ca@gmail.com